TREE SHAKER

D0561744

A **New York Times** BOOK

TREE SHAKER

The Story of Nelson Mandela

Bill Keller

SQUARE
FISH

ROARING BROOK PRESS
New York

Page 1 photo: Nelson Mandela speaks in Soweto after his release from prison in February 1990.

Page 2 photo: President Bill Clinton and Nelson Mandela look out from the jail cell where Mandela spent eighteen years; March 1998.

SQUARE
FISH

An Imprint of Macmillan
175 Fifth Avenue
New York, NY 10010
macteenbooks.com

TREE SHAKER. Copyright © 2008 by The New York Times.
All rights reserved. Printed in the United States of America by
R. R. Donnelley & Sons Company, Harrisonburg, Virginia.

Square Fish and the Square Fish logo are trademarks of Macmillan and
are used by Roaring Brook Press under license from Macmillan.

Square Fish books may be purchased for business or promotional use. For
information on bulk purchases, please contact the Macmillan Corporate and Premium
Sales Department at (800) 221-7945 x5442 or by e-mail at
specialmarkets@macmillan.com.

LIBRARY OF CONGRESS CATALOGING-IN-PUBLICATION DATA

KELLER, BILL.
TREE SHAKER / BILL KELLER.
P. CM.
INCLUDE BIBLIOGRAPHICAL REFERENCES AND INDEX
ISBN 978-1-59643-533-9
1. MANDELA, NELSON, 1918 JUVENILE LITERATURE.   2. PRESIDENTS—
SOUTH AFRICA BIOGRAPHY—JUVENILE LITERATURE.   I. TITLE.
DT1974.K45 2008
968.06'5092 DC22
[B]
2007003559

First published in hardcover by Kingfisher Publications, LLC.
First American Square Fish Edition: 2013
Book designed by Nik Keevil, keevildesign.co.uk
Photo research by Cee Weston-Baker and Maggie Berkvist
Square Fish logo designed by Filomena Tuosto

10 9 8 7 6 5 4 3 2 1

AR: 9.5 / LEXILE: 1270L

Please Note
Throughout this book, you will see symbols (left) that include a page number.
Follow these symbols to the back of the book to read articles and excerpts that
were published in The New York Times. These stories provide more detail and
background to important events in the text. (The symbols at the back of the
book above each article will direct you back to the relevant main text.)

To my pride (Tom, Molly, and Alice)
and joy (Emma)

Durban residents line up to cast
their votes, April 27, 1994.

CONTENTS

About seven miles off the coast of Cape Town, South Africa, sits a windswept lump of shale and limestone known as Robben Island.

THE OLD MEN

ver the centuries since Dutch explorers colonized this region at the southern tip of Africa, the island has been a place for outcasts—an exile for defeated African warriors, a leper colony, a lunatic asylum. For most of those years, it was a prison.

One day in February 1994, a ferry splashed through choppy seas carrying the island's most famous former prisoner, Nelson Mandela. Five of his old prison mates, a documentary filmmaker, and a crowd of journalists accompanied him.

The first time Mandela had traveled to Robben Island, in 1963, he had sat below the decks of the wooden ferry, chained hand and foot. The guards above amused themselves by urinating through the air vent onto the prisoners.

This time, Mandela was treated as a dignitary. He was seventy-five years old and had spent more than twenty-seven of those years in prisons, without losing an ounce of spirit. He was tall and stiff as a flagpole. He had a mouth usually turned down in a kind of mournful frown and brown eyes that often seemed filled with mischief.

Mandela had started life as a child of royalty, had become the country's most notorious outlaw, and was now an emblem of moral courage around the globe.

South Africa was nearing the most thrilling moment in its history. For more than three hundred years, a minority of whites had gotten their way in this naturally abundant land. For the past half a century, whites had ruled under a bizarre system called apartheid, which stripped nonwhites of power and dignity by treating them as aliens in their own land. The cruelties of this arrangement led to violent unrest in the country and made South Africa a popular horror story around the world.

All of this was about to change, not through a bloody revolution, but through an election. I was covering this miracle for *The New York Times*. It was a captivating assignment, because it was a story of democracy struggling to be born, and because it had at its center one of the world's most charismatic figures.

This visit to Robben Island was an election campaign stunt, the kind of staged event reporters usually hate. But none of us complained as we were herded from one photo opportunity to another. The day felt charged with history and symbolism. Soon South African blacks, for so long denied a voice in their own government, would be allowed to cast the first votes of their lives, and the former outcasts would be running the country.

It was hard to imagine, watching Mandela and his former cell mates explore the scene of their captivity, that the white South African government had once regarded these old men as dangerous terrorists. Govan Mbeki, the oldest of the group, was now eighty-three. With his wispy hair and owlish glasses, he looked like a

Aerial view of Robben Island with Cape Town in the background.

retired professor. The youngest, Ahmed Kathrada, was sixty-four years old now—the son of immigrants from India, he was a thoughtful man who had earned multiple college degrees while in prison. As the six men swapped memories and hammed it up for photographers, they seemed like senior citizens on a field trip.

Yet these men had been defendants together in one of the great courtroom dramas of the twentieth century. They had been found guilty of plotting to overthrow the apartheid government by force—in fact, they had proudly admitted to the crime and narrowly escaped being hanged.

When they were sentenced to prison for life, an editorial in *The New York Times* called them "the George Washingtons and Ben Franklins of South Africa."

90

For several hours we toured the island by bus and listened to the former inmates describe the drudgery and petty humiliations of prison routine. We drove to the limestone quarry, where they had spent their days in the dust and glare, crushing stone to be used for road gravel. A cameraman persuaded the old boys to stand together in the brilliant sunshine and sing one of the liberation songs that helped them pass the days of hard labor. Then we rode to their old cell block, where Mandela posed for pictures in his cell—a cage so narrow that when Mandela, who is over six feet tall, had stretched out on his straw mat to sleep, his feet touched one wall and his head grazed the other.

The former prisoners were welcomed by the new prison commander with a nervous smile and a meal of chicken and vegetables in the VIP guesthouse, and then Mandela held a press conference. His campaign advisers had told him that on this day—at the height of an election campaign—the world was hungry for stories of his suffering and endurance. And so, in a sad, husky voice, tears brimming in his eyes, he talked of his anguish when prison guards brought him the news that his mother had died and then, the following year, that his son had been killed in an auto accident. He had pleaded for permission to attend their funerals, but it was denied.

Nelson Mandela (third from left) and fellow Rivonia trial ex-convicts revisit the lime quarry where the Robben Island prisoners worked. The man second from right is Walter Sisulu.

In 1994, Nelson Mandela revisited the Robben Island jail cell where he had been imprisoned.

Mandela spoke of the hurt and helplessness he and his compatriots had felt knowing their wives and children were being harassed, expelled from jobs and schools, exiled or imprisoned. He described how after the government would impose some new suffering on his family, a mean-spirited guard would leave a newspaper clipping about it in Mandela's cell, just to rub it in.

"That was very painful," Mandela recalled. "Of course, wounds which cannot be seen are more painful than the ones that you can see, which can be cured by a doctor."

The truth is, though, that Mandela and his comrades were not much interested in describing the torments of prison life. On the contrary, they talked with cheerful nostalgia about their days on Robben Island. In prison, they told us, they had studied and argued and debated. They plotted escapes and swapped messages in invisible ink. They honed their tactics for dealing with white authority, and they created an old-boy network that would remain an essential source of strength long after their release. Ahmed Kathrada told me that now that they were free men, they sometimes missed the time for leisurely thought and discussion they had enjoyed in prison.

I realized, watching these gentle grandfathers laughing over their memories, that Robben Island was not just their prison. It had been their university. They had graduated from this place ready to change the world. And now the old men were about to finish their work.

Aerial view of Robben Island Prison, off Cape Town.

Nelson Mandela, June 2005.

For centuries, white conquerors from Europe had established colonies in Africa, seeking cotton, coffee, tea, and minerals for their citizens back home, opening new markets for their manufactured goods, and enlarging their empires.

CHAPTER 1

BLACK & WHITE

In many parts of the continent, the invaders brought weapons and disease. The original inhabitants were robbed of their land and livestock, divided into make-believe countries by foreign mapmakers, and subjected to the rule of white administrators (or blacks who followed their orders). Africans who were shipped to Europe and the Americas endured slavery, segregation, and all manner of injustice and humiliation. Blacks

A 1676 engraving of ships in Cape Town harbor, with Table Mountain in the background.

in South Africa suffered all these cruelties and were also subjected to a unique system of oppression put into place in the twentieth century. White South Africans invented a monstrous contraption of laws, maps, and language, designed to reduce the Africans to the status of foreigners in their own land. This was the system Nelson Mandela devoted his life to dismantling.

• • •

The modern history of South Africa begins in the middle of the seventeenth century, when Dutch sailors who worked for the world's most powerful global trading company, the Dutch East India Company, landed in a harbor near the southern tip of Africa. The company had risen to power transporting valuable spices, silk, and cotton from Asia to Europe. This required sending fleets of trading ships on a perilous journey around the rugged and stormy southern end of Africa—the Cape of Good Hope. Searching for a place where the boats could stock up on supplies before continuing around the cape, the Dutch found the port that would become Cape Town. It is one of the most beautiful harbors on earth, with glistening beaches and a towering pedestal of rock and greenery called Table Mountain.

Before the Europeans arrived, South Africa had only been

Illustration showing Willem Adriaan van der Stel, Dutch governor of the Cape Colony, with slaves on his farm in South Africa, ca. 1780.

populated by three native groups. Roving bands of hunters, known as the San, pursued abundant herds of antelope, zebras and elephants, rhinoceros, lions, and leopards. The Khoikhoi were sheep and cattle herders. Farther inland, more settled communities farmed the land and raised livestock. They included a variety of tribes and kingdoms—the Zulu, the Xhosa (Mandela's people), the Sotho, and the Tswana, among others. Historians refer to this group as Bantu-speakers, because their languages had much in common, or simply Africans.

The little Dutch supply post in Cape Town expanded. Colonists arrived, and slaves were brought in to do the hard labor. Some of the slaves were from Africa, but most were from India, Indonesia, Ceylon, and other Asian countries. As a result, South Africa today—especially Cape Town—has a mix of races and religions unlike any other place on earth.

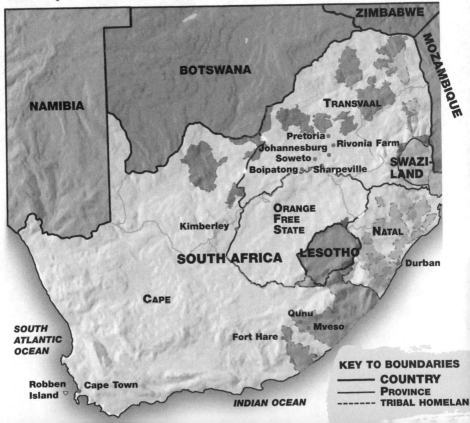

For the native herdsmen, the arrival of the whites was a catastrophe. The new settlers pushed them aside, taking over their pastures and their herds and beginning centuries of intermittent warfare between whites and blacks.

Khoikhoi who were suspected of theft were branded with hot irons and dumped on Robben Island. A smallpox infection brought by the Europeans nearly annihilated the herdsmen.

Zulu war dance in an undated photograph, Natal, South Africa.

Seeking better farmland and grazing lands, the colonists moved east and north. During this period, the Dutch settlers began referring to themselves as Afrikaners. In their minds, they were the first real Africans, the ones entitled to rule the land, even though the natives had been there for centuries.

At the end of the 1700s, the British, who had become the dominant world power, took control of Cape Town. Like the Dutch, they intended to use it as a base on the way to and from Asia. But gradually the British, too, began expanding their domain, pushing into the territories of both the Afrikaners and the Africans.

The first settled African population the whites encountered was the Xhosa people, who fought back when the Europeans invaded their land. But the Xhosa were overcome not only by European guns but also by two invisible weapons—disease and superstition. First a scourge of lung disease wiped out many of the Xhosa cattle herds. Then a teenage girl regarded as a prophetess predicted that if the Xhosa slaughtered their remaining cattle and destroyed their grain,

the ghosts of their ancestors would rise from the dead and restore them to power. Some of the leading chiefs believed this vision, and after the destruction was carried out, many thousands of Xhosa died of starvation.

As they pushed farther east, whites encountered the vast Zulu kingdom, which had been formed when many rival clans were united by the military prowess of a chief named Shaka. Shaka is remembered mainly as a ruthless warrior—according to Zulu lore, he once kidnapped the mother of a rival chief and locked her in her house overnight with a pack of jackals, who devoured her alive. But when the Europeans arrived, Shaka tried to buy peace by giving them rights to build homes and farms on Zulu land. Shaka's successors, however, fought many battles against both the Afrikaners and the British.

The white conquest proceeded in a series of advances and retreats. The Africans had vastly superior numbers—whites never exceeded 20 percent of the population—but the blacks were divided, had inferior weapons, and had no natural immunity to the diseases that arrived with the Europeans.

Although some of the colonizers saw themselves as benefactors to the Africans, providing them with education, religion, or economic assistance, most of the whites were openly racist. Their goal was to push the Africans off the most desirable land and contain them on reservations. The Afrikaners were especially rigid in their racial views, but the British—who tended to pride themselves on being more enlightened and even allowed a limited vote to blacks in Cape Colony— quickly adopted the attitude of the Afrikaners.

"Virtually all the Whites in the region, in common with their contemporaries in Europe and the Americas, regarded themselves as belonging to a superior, Christian, civilized race and believed that, as such, they were justified in appropriating native land, controlling native labor, and subordinating native authorities," the historian Leonard Thompson wrote.

A miner holds the Cullinan Diamond shortly after it was found ca. 1907. After cutting, it was used for the British Crown and Scepter.

European interest in South Africa intensified in 1870, when miners digging around the town of Kimberley, near the very middle of South Africa, found that the dry soil was veined with diamonds. It was the richest diamond discovery in history. Then, in 1886, on a plateau farther east, where Johannesburg is located today, diggers found vast reefs of gold.

The diamonds and gold attracted shiploads of prospectors. And it meant the Africans had a new role. After all, someone had to do the backbreaking, dangerous work of digging out this astounding mineral wealth.

91

Whites were given good jobs as supervisors. Many black men were sent to crouch in the mines, picking minerals from a rock face in boiling heat. Leaving their families behind in the designated African areas, the black laborers lived in all-male barracks, where they slept fifty to a room, racked like wine bottles in bunks made of concrete. Whites were free to travel, but blacks were confined to their migrant labor camps and required to carry passes wherever they went. This system, with its segregated territories and pass laws, would later become the model for apartheid.

Whites fought not only with Africans but with each other,

Workers in the De Beers Diamond Mines, Kimberley, South Africa, ca. 1940s.

especially when the immense bounty of diamonds and gold entered the picture. The British and Afrikaners frequently clashed and even fought two wars, known as the Boer Wars, from 1880 to 1881 and 1899 to 1902. In the end the British triumphed, putting down Afrikaner guerrilla fighters with the use of brutal tactics, such as herding civilians into prison camps where thousands, mostly children, died of disease. Relations between British South Africans and Afrikaners remain strained to this day.

In 1910 British and Afrikaner colonists finally united, forming the Union of South Africa, with English and Dutch as the official languages. Virtually all the power was in the hands of whites.

They used this power to keep blacks separate and subservient. Under laws enacted by the new national parliament, Africans could own property only in specific reserves, usually the poorest land. The government built roads and railroads but bypassed the native territories, leaving them isolated. Generous government loans were granted to white farmers but rarely to Africans.

The African homelands became squalid places—dirt-poor, overcrowded, hungry. Children often died young. As blacks were drawn to the cities by mining and factory jobs, they were confined to urban locations called townships, rough black ghettos where domestic workers and manual laborers could live while serving the more affluent white neighborhoods.

The miserable conditions in the black homelands and townships gave rise to reformers pushing for equality—or at least for more humane treatment of the Africans. White missionaries opened Christian schools and colleges, which became the only places black children could get a modern education. Black mine workers organized trade unions to demand better conditions, but they were suppressed. When African workers tried to win concessions by refusing to work, the government responded with violence and arranged to import thousands of workers from China to take their places.

One of the most important liberation movements of modern history began in 1893 when a railroad conductor kicked a young

Indian lawyer out of a first-class train compartment that was reserved for whites. The insulted lawyer began a campaign to overturn laws that discriminated against the Indian minority in South Africa. He took little interest in Africans, but he forged South Africa's first nonwhite political resistance out of Indian plantation workers and merchants. After twenty-one frustrating years, he returned home to India to lead a more successful opposition that eventually ended British colonial rule in that country.

The lawyer, whose name was Mohandas K. Gandhi, is remembered as one of the greatest moral crusaders in modern history. Although Gandhi did not focus on the specific rights of Africans, his belief in the power of nonviolent protest strongly influenced civil rights groups that followed.

In the first half of the twentieth century, though, organizations supporting racial equality posed no real threat to white supremacy in South Africa. And the government was intent on keeping things that way. While some whites argued for a more moderate course, the Afrikaner-led National Party demanded even stricter separation of the races, firm white control of the police and military, and ruthless suppression of anyone who challenged the existing order.

92

Three generations of Boer (Dutch) fighters in 1900: P. J. Lemmer, age sixty-five, J.D.L. Botha, age fifteen, and G. J. Pretorius, age forty-three.

A boy bringing home firewood to cook meals in Transkei, South Africa, ca. 1950.

He was not called "Nelson" until he was seven. A schoolteacher, following colonial tradition, gave the Mandela boy that name on his first day of classes, probably in honor of the great British naval commander Admiral Lord Nelson.

TREE SHAKER

T he name his parents gave him at birth, Rolihlahla, was the Xhosa word for "tree shaker." Later in life Mandela enjoyed pointing out that his people use the word to mean "troublemaker."

Rolihlahla Mandela was born on July 18, 1918, in Mvezo, a tiny village alongside the Mbashe River in the hills of a southern province called Transkei. His father, Gadla Henry Mphakanyiswa, was a chief of the Left-Hand House of the Thembu tribe, a minor branch of the tribe that traditionally produced advisers to the tribal rulers. Gadla served as the village headman in Mvezo, performing marriages, funerals, and other ceremonies and receiving a stipend from the British colonial authorities for making sure the locals paid their taxes. He had four wives, who gave birth to four sons and nine daughters.

When Mandela was still an infant, Gadla, known as a stubborn man, got into an argument with the white authorities and refused an order to appear before the colonial magistrate. For his insubordination, he was stripped of his job and most of his land and cattle. Suddenly facing poverty, he sent young Mandela and his mother to the village of Qunu, where relatives could help support them.

The village where Mandela spent his boyhood sat in rolling hills where cattle and sheep grazed. It was a place that had changed little in hundreds of years, about as far away from the noise of the modern world as you could get. Mandela grew up in the family's cluster of beehive-shaped huts made of mud-brick walls and grass roofs, with simple earthen floors and mats for sleeping. He wore a red blanket wrapped around him as a robe. Meals consisted of cornmeal mush, beans and pumpkin from the neighboring gardens, and milk from the family cows. His father, who divided his time among his four wives, was a stern figure when he was at home, but the boy had a large family of uncles, aunts, and cousins to help look out for him.

At age five Mandela joined the other village boys in tending the sheep and calves that made up the villagers' most important wealth. When they were not herding the animals from pasture to pasture, the boys staged stick fights, caught small birds to roast over fires, and swam in the icy streams.

"It is a place where every stone, every blade of grass, every noise made by insects is part of me," Mandela recalled many years later on a visit to Qunu.

Native huts near Dundee in Transkei, South Africa, ca. 1950.

When he was seven, he donned a cutoff pair of his father's trousers and began attending classes in the one-room mission schoolhouse in Qunu. In a village where many residents shunned the Christian school as foreign, Mandela took his first small step on a journey to the modern world.

Two years later, his father died and young Nelson's life took yet another sharp turn. As the descendant of royalty he was invited into the home of his cousin, the acting paramount chief of the Thembu, in Mqhekezweni. It took Mandela and his mother most of a day, walking across hills and valleys, to reach the royal residence. The Great Place, as it was called, was a compound of houses and huts painted a dazzling white, surrounded by gardens, cornfields, and peach and eucalyptus trees. To Western eyes it was not an impressive settlement, but to a boy from a tiny village, Mandela later recalled, it seemed "a magical kingdom."

Around the fire at the Great Place, Mandela listened to stories of the long-ago Xhosa battles against the white invaders, of the great Xhosa cattle slaughter that cost so many lives, of the Xhosa warriors who stood up to the Europeans. His first heroes were leaders of Xhosa resistance who had been banished by the British to Robben Island.

In later years, tribal identity would not be something younger members of the African National Congress talked about. Apartheid, which used the tribal system as an excuse to keep Africans separate and powerless, had made the whole idea of tribes seem shameful to some blacks. But Mandela would always remember his upbringing in the royal court with affection, and understand the powerful role that tribal attachments played in South Africa.

Almost everyone I met who knew Mandela well traced some aspect of his character back to his royal upbringing: his rather formal bearing, his respect for tradition, his judicial temperament, his regal self-confidence. In his autobiography, Mandela remembers listening in on debates of the tribal council and noticing that the chief often operates the way a shepherd does. "He stays behind the flock, letting the most nimble go out ahead, whereupon the others follow, not realizing that all along they are being directed from behind," he

A Xhosa boy with painted face at manhood initiation rite, Eastern Cape Province, South Africa, ca. 2002.

wrote. Although he would later lead a movement that prized group decisions, Mandela sometimes showed a chiefly willingness to decide matters without consulting others.

As a member of the royal household, a part of the official African elite, Mandela began to dress in Western clothes. He attended the Methodist church and applied himself to the study of English, Xhosa, history, and geography at the mission school. His best friend, Justice, was the paramount chief's son and heir to the palace, and Mandela idolized him. Four years older than Mandela, Justice was handsome, fun-loving, excellent at sports and ballroom dancing, and a bit of a playboy.

At age sixteen, Mandela went through the most important transition of a Xhosa boy's life—circumcision, a ritual that lasted several weeks and marked the formal passage to manhood. Along with Justice and other adolescents, Mandela was taken to a secluded hut for days of preparation. Then, with parents and relatives all looking on, the initiates sat on blankets while a tribal surgeon went from boy to boy, slicing off the foreskin with a razor-sharp blade.

The boys were expected to show no sign of fear or pain—not so much as a frown—until the cut was made and each shouted, "Ndiyindoda!" ("I am a man!").

The boys then limped back to the isolation huts, painted their bodies with white chalk, and waited for the wounds to heal before emerging for gifts and celebration.

Mandela recalled that at the crucial moment he embarrassed himself by acting less brave than the other boys. "I felt as if fire was shooting through my veins; the pain was so intense that I buried my chin into my chest," he wrote later. "Many seconds seemed to pass before I remembered the cry, and then I recovered and called out 'Ndiyindoda!'"

From the day he moved into the Great Place, Mandela's future as a tribal leader was laid out before him. When he finished his instruction at the one-room primary school next to the royal residence, he was sent to the Methodist boarding schools, where he had his first close encounters with whites—the headmasters—and befriended Africans from other tribal backgrounds. His world was widening beyond the boundaries of Xhosa tradition. He was not a brilliant student, but he was diligent, and finally, at the age of twenty, he won admission to the pinnacle of the mission school system, the South African Native College at Fort Hare.

Mandela attended the South African Native College in Fort Hare.

For South African blacks, Fort Hare was a unique opportunity, the gateway to wealth and prestige. For Mandela, it was the place where he truly began to earn his birth name, Tree Shaker.

At first, he adapted easily. He studied law, joined the drama society, competed at soccer and cross-country running, learned ballroom dancing, and attracted plenty of girlfriends. He joined the Student Christian Association, which sent students out on Sundays to teach religion and talk to villagers about sanitation and other concerns.

Near the end of his second year at Fort Hare, the students organized a protest against the dreary food in the dining hall. Mandela resigned from the student council in sympathy and refused to change his mind even when the principal threatened to expel him. He was sent home for summer vacation to reconsider.

Looking back, Mandela called his behavior "foolhardy." After summer vacation, he probably would have apologized and returned to school. But when he reached home, he got a terrible surprise. The chief had arranged for him to be married. Indeed, brides had already been selected for both Mandela and his cousin Justice, and the double wedding was already scheduled.

The young woman selected for Mandela was the daughter of a Thembu priest. She was rather fat, and Mandela knew her to be secretly in love with Justice. In any case, Mandela was not ready to settle down, especially with a bride he did not love.

So, when the chief was away on business, Mandela and Justice tricked a local trader into giving them money for two of the royal oxen and they fled. After a series of misadventures, they made their way to Soweto, the vast black slum beside the gold-mining metropolis of Johannesburg. A few days earlier, Mandela had been a college student bound for a traditional life in tribal government. Now he was a country boy in the rough city, without legal travel papers, cut off from his furious guardian, his education abandoned and the money he had stolen from the chief almost gone.

Like thousands of blacks before them, Justice and Mandela found work in the gold mines—Justice as a clerk, Mandela in the lowly position of a night watchman, patrolling the segregated mining compound with a whistle and nightstick. Before long, the tree shaker got in trouble with his bosses and was fired. A cousin sent him to see a real estate agent named Walter Sisulu. A short, confident man, Sisulu was also the local kingpin of the African National Congress, an organization that had been founded in 1912 by a group of educated African lawyers to promote the cause of racial equality.

Many years later, I went to see Sisulu, who was then one of Mandela's dearest friends, to ask him about the young man who showed up that day in his real estate office. He thought back to their first meeting, how he looked upon the visitor—a

Walter Sisulu, May 1962.

towering young man with aristocratic cheekbones, utterly self-assured—and decided his prayers had been answered.

"I had no hesitation, the moment I met him, that this is the man I need," said Sisulu.

"Needed for what?" I asked.

"For leading the African people," Sisulu said.

And, sure enough, Mandela took Soweto by storm. Sisulu arranged for him to work as a clerk at a law firm while he studied for a law degree. Mandela then connected with a friend from Fort Hare, Oliver Tambo, and together they opened the first black law partnership in South Africa. He took up amateur boxing, rising at four a.m. to go running through the streets of Soweto. He took to wearing fashionable suits. Women loved him. Not long after arriving in the big city, at the Sisulus' house, he met a pretty nurse named Evelyn Mase, and within a few months he proposed. They eventually had three children, including a daughter who died when she was nine months old.

• • •

In 1943, when he was twenty-five, Mandela joined his first political protest, marching with activists of the African National Congress to oppose a fare increase on buses serving a major African township. The ANC had been formed in reaction to the unification of South Africa's British and Afrikaner provinces into a single white-ruled country. The group wrote appeals to the government and organized protests in support of racial equality. But up until the 1940s the ANC had consisted mainly of middle-class African professionals and tribal royalty. It avoided confrontation and attracted little public following. By the time Mandela and his friend Tambo joined, the Congress was beginning to stir to life, and the two men quickly stood out as young leaders.

From the beginning, what struck others about

Mandela in 1952, when he was a partner of Mandela and Tambo Attorneys, Johannesburg.

Nelson Mandela was his absolute confidence that he could win over doubters to his point of view.

"His starting point," Walter Sisulu told me, "is . . . 'I am going to persuade this person no matter what.' That is his gift. He will go to anybody, anywhere, with that confidence. Even when he does not have a strong case, he convinces himself that he has."

At the time, the big debate in black South Africa was over nonracialism versus Africanism. The ANC was open to people of all races and cultivated alliances with white and Indian opposition groups. The Africanists, or black nationalists, argued that before blacks could take their place in a society of many races, they had to rebuild the confidence crushed by generations of oppression. They had to be totally self-sufficient. Mandela, just a few months removed from the Thembu royal palace, became, for a time, an ardent Africanist. Together with militant friends, he disrupted Communist Party meetings because he considered Communism a foreign, white ideology. He insisted the ANC keep its distance from Indian and mixed-race political movements.

Impatient with the cautiousness of the African National Congress, Mandela, Tambo, Sisulu, and other younger militants organized the ANC Youth League in 1944. They announced their plans with a manifesto filled with the angry language of African nationalism—so much so that some of their white and Indian sympathizers were offended.

"I was angry at the white man, not at racism," Mandela recalled later. "While I was not prepared to hurl the white man into the sea, I would have been perfectly happy if he climbed aboard his steamships and left the continent of his own volition."

Five years after founding the Youth League, the young upstarts organized a revolt and took charge of the entire African National Congress. As usual, Mandela was shaking the trees.

A young Nelson Mandela in Johannesburg in the early 1960s.

The formal structure of apartheid was not constructed until Mandela was in his early thirties. In 1948, the Afrikaner-led National Party won elections on a platform of strict separation of the races. What had until then been a slogan now became a national project and an international scandal.

CHAPTER 3

APARTNESS

The great dreamer of apartheid—the word coined by the Afrikaners literally means "apartness"—was Hendrik Frensch Verwoerd. A Dutch psychologist raised in southern Africa, Verwoerd (pronounced fur-VOORT) was an ardent believer in white supremacy and separation of the races. After the National Party came to power he was made minister of native affairs. Later he would become prime minister, presiding over the most merciless period of white rule. It was his regime that would send Nelson Mandela to Robben Island.

Once in power, Verwoerd and his fellow Afrikaners immediately set to work creating a system that would keep the large black majority under control, assure a pool of cheap labor for white-run businesses, and protect against the mixing of the races, which many Afrikaners saw as a threat to their national identity.

In the decade following the National Party victory, the laws that made up the apartheid system were put into place. They were as monstrous in concept as those invented by the Nazis of Germany, whom Verwoerd studied and admired.

The Population Registration Act, enacted in 1950, required that every person be classified by race: white, black, Indian, or "colored," a category that included the mixed-race descendants of Asian slaves and Khoikhoi herders.

A government board was created to oversee the classification process, and vague guidelines were provided to help members in their work. For example, the law defined a "white person" as someone who "in appearance is obviously a white person" or "is generally accepted as a white person."

In other words, if you could produce white witnesses who said they considered you white, you stood a chance of being classified as white. Imagine the humiliation of standing before a grim bureaucrat who would decide your future based on the tint of your skin and shape of your nose. When in doubt, officials would stick a pencil through a person's hair. If the hair was curly enough to hold the pencil, the person was classified as black or colored.

Every other aspect of life in South Africa depended on your classification. The Prohibition of Mixed Marriages Act (1949) decreed that people of different races could not marry. This sometimes meant breaking up families in which the husband and wife had different classifications.

Prime Minister Hendrik F. Verwoerd, a firm believer in South African apartheid laws, speaking in 1960.

The Reservation of Separate Amenities Act (1953) authorized the government to offer segregated and greatly inferior facilities to nonwhites, from maternity wards to cemeteries. Under apartheid, South Africa maintained separate buses with separate bus stops, separate schools, and separate hospitals. The sign NET BLANKES—"whites only"—appeared on taxis and toilets, benches and elevators. White and black sports teams could not compete against one another.

Of course, children of different races were not allowed to share classrooms. The Bantu Education Act (1953)—"Bantu" was the official word for black Africans under apartheid—crippled the missionary education system that had raised Mandela and many other black leaders. This law ensured that black students would be educated by the state, mostly in decrepit, jam-packed, poorly equipped classrooms where the curriculum included plenty of apartheid brainwashing.

Other laws hardened the racial boundaries around living areas. The Group Areas Act (1950) designated separate residential areas for the four racial groups. Africans who found themselves living in the wrong sector were forcibly removed to areas zoned for them. Blacks who were needed in white cities as low-wage laborers were crowded

Black South Africans line up at the counter of a government office to get their passbooks, Johannesburg, April 1960.

into squalid townships and required to carry passes when they traveled in white areas.

Perhaps the weirdest feature of this legal monstrosity was the homeland system. Under the Bantu Authorities Act (1951), the government mapped out ten little black states, or Bantustans, and decreed that these were the tribal homelands of the African population. Most consisted of isolated bits of land, the leftovers after the best farming areas were carved out for whites. Traditional chiefs, often corrupt and authoritarian, were made the rulers of these enclaves and were paid by the government—as long as they followed the apartheid rules. All black people were required to become citizens of the homeland that was assigned to their ethnic group, regardless of whether they had ever lived there.

The plan was to gradually grant these impoverished African zones "independence," meaning they would become not just segregated sectors of South Africa but separate countries. Thus blacks would not just be second-class citizens; they would be citizens of somewhere else altogether. In all, the apartheid laws uprooted an estimated 3.5 million people from their homes— roughly the population of the city of Los Angeles.

As protests arose, the government responded with increasingly harsh security measures. The Suppression of Communism Act (1950) gave the minister of justice the power to banish any group or individual for seeking political or social changes by fomenting "disorder" or for encouraging

A Black South African shows his new passbook, ca. 1960.

"feelings of hostility between the European and non-European races." Anyone named by the minister could be, without further explanation, put under house arrest, prohibited from attending public gatherings, and banned from being quoted in publications. Over the following decades, the suppression of dissent became more and more ruthless. The president was given the power to declare a state of emergency, which allowed police to arrest people and put them in jail indefinitely without a trial.

Members of banned political groups were locked in solitary confinement, tortured, and sometimes killed.

As the machinery of apartheid grew, so did the opposition. In 1952, the African National Congress sent the government an ultimatum demanding a repeal of major apartheid laws and threatening a national campaign of nonviolent resistance. (The campaign was modeled on the example of the Indian lawyer Mohandas K. Gandhi, who had returned to India some years earlier and helped win his country's independence from Britain in 1947.) Mandela argued for an Africans-only protest, but his ANC comrades insisted on including Indian and white antiapartheid groups.

Mandela was assigned a major role—recruiting volunteers to flout the apartheid laws by boarding railroad cars reserved for whites or

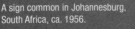

A sign common in Johannesburg, South Africa, ca. 1956.

parading in the streets after curfew. Mandela himself was arrested for a curfew violation—his first taste of a jail cell. The Defiance Campaign, of course, did not bring an end to apartheid. If anything, it made the authorities more ironfisted than ever. But it transformed the ANC from a cautious elite into a popular movement. It also convinced Mandela that the fight against apartheid would be more successful—and have greater moral authority—if it embraced people of all races. His Africanist period was over.

As the government cracked down harder, frustration grew. Mandela, in 1953, became one of the first ANC leaders to argue that they should change tactics, from peaceful civil disobedience to armed insurrection—that is, revolt with weapons. Even after his colleagues rejected a turn to violence, Mandela on his own arranged a mission to China to seek arms for the cause. (The Chinese said no.)

When he was not working for the ANC, Mandela still practiced law with Oliver Tambo. Their business flourished as they represented African clients in white-run courts, work that exposed them almost

daily to the insults and racial hostility of white magistrates and witnesses. Mandela developed a reputation for fearlessness and showmanship. His court appearances often drew black spectators eager to watch him joust with white prosecutors and judges.

In 1956, the ANC organized a conference of opposition groups in order to adopt a declaration of principles called the Freedom Charter. The charter advocated equal status for people regardless of race, free education and medical care, and public ownership of the mines, banks, and big industry. In a free country, the document would have been regarded as harmless; in South Africa, the effect was explosive. In December, Mandela and scores of others were arrested. The government contended that the Defiance Campaign and the Freedom Charter amounted to a conspiracy to overthrow the government. The charge was high treason. The penalty was death. The trial would stretch on for more than four years before the accused were acquitted.

The defendants were free on bail for most of that time, but the legal defense and the activities of the

Nelson Mandela sings with supporters and the accused during the first treason trial in Johannesburg in 1956.

ANC consumed Mandela's time and attention. His law business collapsed, and so did his marriage. The demands of the antiapartheid movement meant Mandela was rarely at home. ("Where does Daddy live?" one of his children asked when Mandela disappeared for yet another organizing trip.) His flirtations with other women and Evelyn's conversion to the Jehovah's Witnesses—a religion that rejects involvement in politics—strained the relationship. Mandela and Evelyn divorced.

Nelson Mandela with his second wife, Winnie, January 1, 1962.

Before long Mandela met a beautiful medical social worker named Nomzamo Winifred Madikizela, known as Winnie. She was sixteen years younger than and somewhat in awe of this township hero. Mandela was immediately smitten and announced on their first date that he would marry her. A year later, in 1958, while the treason trial was still grinding on, they married.

Even though Mandela and Winnie created two daughters and clearly loved each other, there was never much doubt that Mandela was married first of all to the movement. He was often on the road, and when he was home, their family sleep would sometimes be interrupted by police raids and searches of their house.

Year by year, the tension between the white rulers and the black resistance escalated. In 1960, a nationalist group called the Pan-Africanist Congress, a rival of the ANC, announced a day of protest in black townships. The police fired on peaceful protesters in the township of Sharpeville, killing sixty-nine. Black leaders responded by organizing nationwide strikes and marches. The government declared a state of emergency and outlawed the ANC, the Pan-Africanist Congress, and other antiapartheid organizations. Now tempers were raging.

Finally, in March 1961, the court dismissed the treason charges against Mandela and the other defendants. After years of inept witnesses, fabricated evidence, and courtroom theater, the judge ruled that there was no proof the ANC favored violent revolution.

The trial increased Mandela's reputation. It also put him at the top of the government's enemies list. So after the victory in court, he went underground, living in hideouts, moving in disguise from town to town, meeting comrades in secret to avoid another arrest. He delighted in eluding roadblocks and popping up at public events, then calling newspaper reporters to boast of how he and his comrades had outsmarted the police.

Mandela finally persuaded the ANC leadership to endorse armed struggle. Mandela himself was named the first commander in chief of a new rebel army, Spear of the Nation.

"For me," Mandela wrote later, "nonviolence was not a moral principle but a strategy; there is no moral goodness in using an ineffective weapon."

The ANC's army would never be a mighty force. Its military activities consisted mainly of blowing up electrical stations and water mains, planting explosives under police cars, giving hand grenades to township youngsters, and performing occasional acts of terror against civilians. In the most notorious case, in 1986, a mixed-race saboteur named Robert McBride wrapped bullets and metal scraps around one hundred pounds of explosives, hid the bomb in a car, and parked it between two crowded bars in the city of Durban. Three women were killed and sixty-nine people were wounded in the attack.

During his underground days, Mandela became a figure of legend in the townships. He was called "the Black Pimpernel," a twist on a character from a famous French adventure novel about a mysterious hero named the Scarlet Pimpernel. In fact, as Mandela himself would say, most of the stories about his underground exploits were exaggerated. Although he recruited the leaders for the new ANC guerrilla army and traveled to other African countries seeking support, Mandela's days as an outlaw apparently included no outright acts of violence. The exploits of the Black Pimpernel came to an abrupt end when he drove into a police ambush in 1962 and was, again, arrested.

The climactic legal drama of Mandela's life was called the Rivonia Trial, named for the farm where the defendants had allegedly plotted a violent campaign to bring down the apartheid regime. Mandela and eight comrades were accused of a conspiracy to overthrow the state.

The defendants had little hope of winning the case. After all, there were documents, many in Mandela's handwriting, that laid out plans to topple the government. Mandela proposed to his colleagues that they turn the court into a theater to impress the cruelty of the apartheid system upon the world. They even agreed among themselves that if they were sentenced to hang, they would not appeal the verdict but would go to their deaths to shock the world.

On the first day of the trial, Mandela startled the courtroom by arriving in the traditional leopard-skin cloak of Xhosa royalty to dramatize the fact that he was an African entering a white man's court.

Mandela's speech in his defense lasted four hours. He began by describing his own evolution from tribal child to black nationalist to a believer that societies should treat all races equally. He admitted that the defendants had organized a liberation army and committed acts of sabotage—but said these acts were justified because all other paths to democracy were closed off.

His closing words to the court are regarded as such an eloquent summary of his creed that, many years later, they were played to crowds at his campaign rallies.

"I have fought against white domination, and I have fought against black domination," he told the court. "I have cherished the ideal of a democratic and free society in which all persons will live together in harmony and with equal opportunities. It is an ideal which I hope to live for and see realized. But if it need be, my lord, it is an ideal for which I am prepared to die."

They were found guilty, as they knew they would be. Under great pressure from liberals at home and abroad, including a resolution passed by the United Nations General Assembly, the judge spared them the death penalty and sentenced them all to life in prison.

Mandela was forty-four years old when he entered prison. He would be seventy-one when he was released.

Winnie Mandela with her children and Nelson Mandela's mother outside the Palace of Justice during the Rivonia Trial, December 1963.

A typical cell in Robben Island Prison as it is today. The prison was made a historical museum in 1996.

Robben Island Prison was apartheid in miniature. The wardens were all white. (White convicts were confined in separate prisons on the mainland.)

CHAPTER 4

ROBBEN ISLAND UNIVERSITY

Asian and colored prisoners were issued long trousers and shoes with socks, and they got bread with their meals and more generous servings of sugar in their tea. Black prisoners wore boyish short pants and shoes without socks, and they received stingier food rations. After their days laboring in the stone quarry, the inmates slept on cold straw mats in cells furnished with a few thin blankets and iron buckets for toilets. Mandela stocked his cell with books but left his green walls bare. "I have never believed in decorating cells," he told reporters on the day we visited Robben Island.

Just as Robben Island was a small replica of the racial order imposed in South Africa, for Mandela and his fellow inmates the prison sentences were a continuation of resistance. From the day they arrived, they set out to challenge authority, using a combination of protest, negotiation, and subterfuge. Mandela understood that his captors believed themselves to be civilized men, men of laws—not savages. Drawing on his legal training, he found he could often use their own rules against them. He recognized, too, that although some of the guards were brutal, most of them were human and could be touched by courtesy, flattery, and charm.

Soon after arriving at Robben Island, Mandela demanded to see the head of the prison to protest the fact that black inmates were given short pants. After two weeks of listening to Mandela argue his case, the prison commander relented. Mandela found a pair of long pants dumped on the floor of his cell. But when he learned long pants had not been issued to any of the other black prisoners, he refused to wear them. The warden was confounded by this behavior, but Mandela persisted until all of the inmates were offered long pants.

Although the prisoners were supposed to be isolated from one another and the outside world, they quickly developed an elaborate communications system. Mandela and other imprisoned leaders of the African National Congress formed an ANC unit in the cell block. They quietly arranged study groups to teach their beliefs to a population that, at times, totaled more than one thousand political prisoners.

The inmates introduced protest tactics they had employed before their imprisonment. They staged work slowdowns at the rock quarry. They would refuse to eat for days on end, knowing the authorities would face international scandal if a well-known political prisoner died of starvation. Mandela realized, as he later noted in his book *Long Walk to Freedom*, "while we did not run the island, the authorities could not run it without us."

Over the years, the prisoners gradually won many concessions. The food improved. They were given freedom to wander in the prison courtyard and gained access to books. They managed to get some of the more vicious guards transferred off the island. After thirteen years of protest, prison officials agreed to end the grueling daily labors in the quarry. Mandela was allowed to plant a garden, where he grew tomatoes, onions, and chilies. Amazingly, by the time he left Robben Island, the guards had set up a tennis court for the prisoners and allowed them to watch movies.

Self-control was power in prison, and Mandela was especially amazing in his ability to master his emotions. Ahmed Kathrada, who was jailed with Mandela, told me that because Mandela kept his feelings to himself, he was respected and admired but not as warmly loved as another older and more approachable political prisoner, Mandela's friend Walter Sisulu. Inmates listened to Mandela, but they confided their fears and sorrows to Sisulu.

"You know the difference between a father and a leader," Kathrada told me. "That was the big difference between them."

The prisoners would later remember the arguing most vividly. Everyone discussed and disputed constantly. During the day, as they labored with their picks and shovels in the quarry, they held whispered debates. At night they scribbled down their thoughts about the issues of the day and smuggled them to one another in matchboxes or hollowed books or even wrapped in plastic and buried in the giant cauldrons of cornmeal mush they were served for supper. The prisoners discovered that they could use milk as invisible ink; the words were unseen when dried but would appear when sprayed with insecticide. In one four-month period, Mandela wrote a five-hundred-page autobiography by napping after dinner, scribbling all night in his cell, then passing his work to another inmate, who copied the text in tiny print and hid the manuscript.

A British journalist took this photograph of Mandela and Sisulu on Robben Island in the early months of their imprisonment.

The prisoners were denied newspapers, magazines, radios, and televisions, but they followed the news by gathering up the scraps of newspaper the guards had used to wrap their sandwiches. Occasionally a friendly guard would leave a newspaper lying in sight. And, of course, every new prisoner who arrived at Robben Island brought fresh information from the world outside the prison.

By the 1970s, the news was exciting: the stern order of apartheid was being shaken by protests, strikes, and acts of sabotage. International debate grew about how to put pressure on the apartheid regime. Black students began to boycott school and march through black townships to protest classes being taught in the Afrikaans language, the language of their oppressor. When authorities used violence to put down the protests—in one case, killing a teenage schoolboy—protests formed at funerals and church services.

This surge of unrest meant new arrests, which in turn meant new waves of political prisoners arriving on Robben Island. The newcomers were different from Mandela and his comrades—they were angry, headstrong, impatient young men who rejected any talk of compromise or negotiation.

South Africans read the newspaper account of a clash between police and black miners at the Western Deep Levels Gold Mine, September 12, 1973.

Many of them were adherents of the Black Consciousness Movement, which stressed black self-reliance and rejected cooperation with whites or other non-Africans. To these militants, Mandela's organization—the African National Congress, which preached racial tolerance—seemed too willing to compromise. The cellblock political discussions grew heated. Mandela, not for the first time—and not for the last—found himself steering a tricky course. He admired the courage of the young militants and recognized them as valuable sources of political energy. Indeed, their zeal reminded him of his younger self. But he was wary of their lack of any practical program for changing the country besides violent rebellion.

After violent clashes in Soweto in June 1976, new incidents broke out in October 1976 between demonstrators and police in Cape Town.

"They used big words—*existentialism, communalism*," Govan Mbeki told me on the day we visited Robben Island. Mbeki was a close friend of Mandela's and the father of the man who would be the country's second black president, Thabo Mbeki. "They talked of blackness. What is there in blackness? That doesn't give you a philosophy." He sounded a little like a father talking about a difficult teenage son.

Ahmed Kathrada said the endless discourse with dissenters at Robben Island prepared the prisoners for their later negotiations with the whites who ruled the country. "It was a great lesson in tolerance," he told me.

Over the ensuing years, Mandela and his fellow ANC leaders won quite a few of the young leaders over to their point of view. It was perhaps Mandela's greatest political gift that he could talk comfortably with almost anyone, from the fiercest black militant to the loudest white racist. In prison he learned the language of the Afrikaners and urged his fellow prisoners to do the same, so they could better understand their white adversaries and argue the case for liberation more clearly. In my time watching him at work, I often marveled at his ability to wear down hostility through endless patience, gentle humor, and charm.

Mandela even charmed his jailers, chatting with them about the state of the country and asking after their families. James Gregory, a warden who censored the prison mail on Robben Island and then guarded Mandela after he was moved to mainland prisons, was invited as an honored guest to Mandela's presidential inauguration. Gregory told reporters that after Mandela was freed from prison, the guard retired out of boredom. "Life had become empty for me," Gregory said.

Mandela, for his part, says his philosophy of nonracialism was reinforced by the behavior of the kinder white guards

100

who treated the inmates sympathetically, smuggling in forbidden newspapers, spooning out extra food rations, and treating visiting relatives with courtesy.

By the early 1980s, the white government was feeling the heat. The unrest in the black townships was making the country difficult to govern. The condemnation from the outside world—other countries sharply disapproved of the blatant oppression in South Africa—was growing, accompanied by boycotts of South African sporting events and threats of economic penalties.

Mandela became a symbol of the resistance to the oppression—at first in South Africa and then around the world. Many of those who were swept up in the cause had little idea who Mandela was. Mandela himself joked later that some of the British protesters carrying signs that said FREE MANDELA! thought "Free" was his first name.

Winnie Mandela, too, lived in the international limelight. For her efforts to carry on the antiapartheid struggle and keep her husband in the public eye, she was arrested, imprisoned for months at a time,

103

Antiapartheid demonstrators in Soweto, June 15, 1980

and constantly harassed. When she persisted in challenging the authorities, she was finally packed into a truck with her furniture and belongings and moved to a barren township three hundred miles from Johannesburg. These torments turned her into something of a liberation celebrity, which helped keep the Mandela name in the international press. But the persecution and isolation also helped turn Winnie, who lacked her husband's patience and diplomatic skills, into a bitter and brutal woman.

If the government was looking for a negotiating partner among the Africans, Nelson Mandela was the obvious candidate. He was the world's most famous political prisoner, the man foreign delegations always asked about and sought to visit. His behavior in prison had established him as someone blacks would follow and someone with whom whites could do business.

In 1982, after eighteen years on Robben Island, Mandela was unexpectedly transferred to Pollsmoor, a prison on the mainland, where he and some of his ANC comrades were given more comfortable quarters. After Robben Island, it was a great luxury—beds with sheets, meals of meat and vegetables, family visits without the glass partition. For the first time in many years, Mandela was allowed to embrace his wife.

After a time, the government began reaching out to Mandela to negotiate. At first he was reluctant, fearing the government would try to use him to calm the unrest in the country without giving up apartheid. He knew, too, that other leaders of the ANC would be furious. They were convinced negotiations would be regarded, both by the government and by Mandela's movement, as a sign of weakness. They insisted there could be no talk of compromise until all political prisoners were freed, troops were withdrawn from black townships, and the crude oppression of apartheid had begun to be dismantled.

And so it was daring, even arrogant, of Mandela to decide—without telling his comrades—that he would negotiate with the government on his own. In 1985, he wrote to the white minister of justice, proposing that they meet to talk about beginning a dialogue. The government, Mandela felt, must have begun to sense that it was on the wrong side of history. Thus began a slow, mutual courtship between the prisoner and his keepers. It would last five years.

Once Mandela and the government decided they could do business with one another, the world's most famous political prisoner was moved to a warden's cottage at Victor Verster Prison, outside of Cape Town. For his final years as a captive, Mandela's home included a garden and swimming pool, a television set with a video player, a cook who baked bread and fixed gourmet meals, and tailor-made suits for his meetings with government luminaries. So luxurious was his place of confinement that some of the ANC officials who came to take part in the secret diplomacy worried that Mandela had sold out to authorities in exchange for privileges.

On February 2, 1990, the newly elected South African president, F. W. de Klerk, stood before a stunned parliament and announced that he was decreeing the beginning of a new world. All political prisoners would be released. Antiapartheid organizations like the ANC, outlawed since 1960, would be unbanned. The state of emergency that had kept black townships under heavy police control for three decades would end. On February 11, 1990, Nelson Mandela walked free. The journey to normalcy could begin.

South African President
F. W. de Klerk in 1990.

When I arrived in South Africa in 1992, the apartheid system was dying. Most of the racist laws had been relaxed. Whites discussed race in a gentler, more diplomatic language, using the word *apartheid* as if it described ancient history.

But South Africa was still two countries. Apartness was a stark reality on the ground.

White South Africa in those days was a place that most Americans or Europeans would find familiar, a land of Toyotas and BMWs on well-paved highways, a nation of shopping malls and steak houses and supermarkets. The nicer suburbs had lush gardens behind tall gates, with signs warning potential intruders that the streets were patrolled by private "armed response" teams. The only blacks in these neighborhoods were maids and gardeners, who lived in little servant quarters in backyards. White schools had small classes, big libraries, well-furnished laboratories, and expansive green sporting fields.

Black South Africa was an altogether different place. Some tidy middle-class enclaves had developed within established black townships such as Soweto. But for most blacks the situation was desperate. Communities located at the outskirts of white cities were crowded, impoverished, and often violent. Black workers' hostels had become havens for criminal gangs. Townships were often surrounded by squatter camps, where the poorest of the poor lived. Some of these places, such as the flatlands outside Cape Town, were oceans of misery, with houses built from scrap, lacking indoor toilets and electricity. The streets were narrow and rutted, thick with mud and sewage in the rainy season and clouded with dust in dry times. These wretched shack towns stretched for miles under a haze of smoke from coal stoves.

In the black schools I visited, teachers often contended with classes of seventy children or more, of varying ages and abilities. They worked from hand-me-down textbooks. There was often a lively spirit—but no microscopes, computers, libraries, maps, soccer balls, or paper.

Even more miserable than the townships were the homelands, those strange make-believe countries invented by apartheid. These tribal reservations were remote and dirt-poor. Fathers were usually away, laboring in the mines or working for other white-owned enterprises. Mothers spent much of the day foraging for firewood and toting jugs of water from distant wells. Children often died young from malnutrition and disease.

Most whites I met in South Africa had never set foot inside a black family's home or even driven through a black township. If they

Villagers in Crossroads Township, Cape Town, 1990.

had visited a homeland, it was probably to enjoy one of the nightclubs or gambling casinos that were built for the entertainment of the more affluent whites. But with the day of majority rule approaching, when blacks would presumably gain control of the government, whites were growing anxious about the collision of the two South African worlds. They worried about the possibility that blacks would turn the tables and expel them from their comfortable homes.

A month before South Africa's first free election, in March 1994, I spent some time in a neighborhood of Johannesburg that had been, before the laws of apartheid took hold, a vibrant multiracial area called Sophiatown. Sophiatown had produced the first black doctor in South Africa, several black lawyers, and a wealth of artistic and political talent. But after winning power in 1948, the National Party removed all fifty-eight thousand of the neighborhood's black residents—luring some away with promises of cheap land, forcing other families onto trucks and moving them to segregated townships. Authorities then bulldozed the black dwellings, fumigated the land, and built little stucco-covered cottages for the Afrikaner middle class. They renamed the area Triomf— **"Triumph."**

Among the residents of this well-tended neighborhood I found a man named Hendrik Verwoerd, the grandson of the prime minister who had expelled the blacks from the area. The younger Verwoerd was not a white supremacist or a politician like his grandfather. He was an insurance salesman and television sports broadcaster, a liberal-minded Afrikaner who admitted that naming the scene of so much black heartbreak "Triumph" was "highly insensitive." Now, like many of his Afrikaner neighbors, he was worried that blacks would view an election victory as a chance to take it all back. That, he insisted, would be unfair.

"Am I to be blamed for something that happened when I was four or five years old?" he asked.

It was a little startling to learn that Verwoerd and his neighbors had placed their hopes in the very man white South Africa had fought so long to keep from power, Nelson Mandela, who had spent much of the election campaign preaching forgiveness and patience. Still, the fear of a black "invasion" was widespread. The residents of Triomf had all heard rumors of black men cruising their streets, checking out their houses and cars, making lists for later.

The interesting thing was that most blacks with whom I spoke expressed no interest in stealing back what was stolen from them. It was rare to encounter blacks who expected instant riches from majority rule. Their dreams rarely included vengeance.

Shortly after visiting Triomf, I spent some time in a field of squatter shacks, one of several black settlements that had been named in honor of the man who would soon be president. The residents of Mandela Park laughed when I remarked that some whites feared that democracy would bring greedy blacks to their doorsteps, demanding cars and mansions.

"What big mansion?" hooted Jack Mokoape, an out-of-work bank teller. "What big mansion, if you can't pay for it? I'm living with people who can think. They know the election doesn't mean then you are going to have a mansion." Of course, a job would be nice, he mused. Or, pointing to the communal water tap he shared with a few hundred others, an indoor faucet. Or perhaps a toilet, a telephone line, or electric lights. But even such modest miracles "will not happen overnight."

"The main thing: I just hope we will be equal," he concluded.

Out in the homelands, some of the black tribal rulers—the corrupt authoritarians who had benefited from apartheid—looked ahead to the free election with deep dread. They were terrified of a new constitution that would dissolve the homeland governments and disband their armies, mostly equipped and maintained by white South Africans. These dictators could sense the end of their power, and some of them vowed to resist.

The first time I visited the supposedly independent state of Ciskei—one of the bogus homelands of the Xhosa people—I thought it was something of a joke. Ciskei was one of four homelands that had achieved full "independence"—but except for South Africa, every country in the world regarded it as still being a part of South Africa. The capital city of Bisho had a tiny "international" airport and a three-block modern downtown, like a toy version of a real city. The government ministers and business executives lived in guarded communities surrounded by countless miles of wretched poverty.

The military dictator of Ciskei, Brigadier Oupa Gqozo, was a short, jumpy man in a general's uniform. He invited me into his office and spent an hour insisting Ciskei was a real country, boiling with rage at any suggestion that he was a puppet of South Africa, controlled by the white government. At that time, Mandela's African National Congress was planning a protest march into Bisho to demand that the homeland be abolished. Brigadier Gqozo was indignant. At one point he leapt from his chair and imitated a high-stepping dance called the toyi-toyi, which is a ritual of political protest in South Africa.

"They are filthy," he said of the ANC. "They are terrible. They are thugs. And they are dangerous."

"I'm not a small boy," he added, when asked about the plans to march on his capital. "I'm going to show them that with me, no is no."

I left that day thinking Ciskei was a sham of a country. Three days later I was back, covering the rally of fifty thousand protesters who marched from the white South African city of Queenstown across the imaginary international border and into the make-believe homeland. The crowd chanted and sang protest songs and danced their toyi-toyi.

Suddenly, from over a rise came the rattle of gunfire and a rain of bullets. Brigadier Gqozo's little army had set up a line of machine guns, and they were firing live ammunition at us.

I dove into the dirt with thousands of others. Later I timed a tape recording of the shooting. The guns blasted away for three minutes, though it seemed longer. When they went silent, twenty-four protest marchers had been killed and scores more were wounded or trampled in the panic.

Apartheid was dying, but it wasn't dead yet.

Protestors in Ciskei run for cover as Gqozo's army opens fire on them; September 1992.

Nelson Mandela casting his
vote in the first democratic
election in South Africa,
April 27, 1994.

When Nelson Mandela walked out of prison in February 1990, few people were confident that South Africa would ever see a free, orderly election with every willing citizen of the country casting a ballot.

CHAPTER 5

THE ROAD TO POWER

Yes, the apartheid system was breaking down under the pressure of black discontent and international condemnation. But what would replace it? And would the change come peacefully or with bloody upheaval?

The men who had decided to free Nelson Mandela understood that they had to give up some of their power or lose it all. But some powerful figures in the government were reluctant to surrender their reign and were determined to sabotage any moves toward majority rule. Africans were divided, too. Some were hungry for a deal that would let them share power with whites, while others were violently opposed to any compromise. And everywhere there were opportunists—black and white—looking to exploit the situation for power, fame, or vengeance.

Like that shepherd patiently moving a flock of sheep, Mandela had to nudge along not only the whites in power, but also his comrades in the antiapartheid movement—even in his own family. Mandela's wife, Winnie, after years of separation from her husband

Nelson Mandela with Walter Sisulu and Winnie Mandela at Bloemfontien rally, February 1990.

and torment by the white government, had become a rabble-rouser. She dressed in military khakis, urged the township youths to perform acts of violence, and surrounded herself with young thugs who terrorized anyone she regarded as an enemy.

When I arrived to begin my journalism assignment in 1992, a strange assortment of South Africans had gathered in a conference center on the outskirts of Johannesburg, struggling to agree on new rules for the country and a date for elections. Mandela and the white president who freed him, F. W. de Klerk, were the leaders of the two main parties, but the gathering included homeland dictators and tribal chiefs, labor union officials and Communist Party members, Indian and mixed-race activists, black nationalists and white separatists—

twenty-six political parties and government bodies in all.

Every detail of the new South Africa had to be worked out: Who would control the army? Would women have equal rights? Would South Africa have a death penalty? What national anthem would the country sing?

As the talks went on, some tried to stop the process by force. One day, as I was wandering through the halls of the massive meeting center, hundreds of white separatists gathered outside the building, armed with pistols and shotguns. As the negotiators inside watched nervously, a man dressed in black drove an armored pickup truck through the huge plate-glass window in the front of the building. After a few fistfights and a lot of shouting, the invaders went home and the talks continued.

A more alarming interruption came when a white extremist gunned down Chris Hani, a young black Communist Party leader who was probably the second most popular activist in the country after Mandela. Hani's murder, in the driveway of his home in a newly integrated suburb, caused an outpouring of anger and mourning.

106

The worst of the bloodshed took place in black townships, where the Inkatha Freedom Party—a Zulu group that was sometimes secretly encouraged by white police—battled supporters of the ANC.

Nelson Mandela and President F. W. de Klerk make opening press statements during the first talks between the South African government and the ANC, May 1990.

In one horrific attack, a band of raiders from a Zulu hostel stormed the black township of Boipatong, slaughtering forty-six people, mainly women and children, with spears and machetes. After hearing about this violence, the ANC walked out of the negotiations, saying the massacre had shattered their trust in the white government, but talks eventually resumed.

Throughout these disruptions, Mandela and de Klerk kept talking. They were an odd couple, partners and rivals at the same time. The two men did not like each other much or trust each other entirely, but they needed each other and they knew it.

"I can never normalize the political situation in this country without him," Mandela told me in an interview during the negotiations. "That is the reality. I would regret if he is overthrown now. I want us to overthrow him properly when we have elections."

Neither man wanted his angry followers to think he was giving in too easily. But both believed deeply that compromise was better than civil war. So de Klerk publicly described Mandela as a "captive" of the Communists and threatened to impose emergency measures to keep the country from sliding into chaos. But he never ordered a police crackdown, and he gradually gave up many of the whites' constitutional demands. In turn, Mandela portrayed de Klerk as dishonest and stubborn and threatened strikes and massive protests. But he stopped short of measures—like a nationwide stop-work campaign—that could scare away foreign companies interested in building factories in South Africa or that might lead to more violence. And he insisted, over the objections of his more radical comrades, that the white minority keep some share of power in the new government. For this patient leadership, Mandela and de Klerk would share the most prestigious honor the world bestows on statesmen, the Nobel Peace Prize.

It took more than eight years if you count from the day Mandela sent word from his prison cell that he was willing to talk. But in

November 1993, the painstaking negotiations produced a constitution, the founding document of a new nation.

The new constitution made many promises. It assured citizens that they would choose their own rulers, enjoy equal rights, experience the freedoms of speech and religion, the right to belong to political groups, and the guarantee of a fair trial. It pledged to disband the horrible homelands. The list of fundamental rights in the new South Africa specifically rejected the abuses of the recent past: There was a prohibition against torture, a promise that people could live where they chose, and an assurance that no one could be stripped of his citizenship. For the majority of people—blacks, treated for so long as foreigners in their own country—the constitution represented their hopes and dreams.

109

Nelson Mandela and F. W. de Klerk pose with their Nobel Peace Prize gold medals and diplomas in Oslo; December 1993.

For the white minority, whose experience and wealth the country could not afford to lose, the constitution offered a large measure of protection. For the first five years, minority political parties would be included in the new government. They would not have a veto over the majority, but they would have a voice. Whites would not be stripped of their property or kicked out of their jobs in the government. In Afrikaner areas, children would be allowed to have classes in their own language. The existing army and the antiapartheid guerrilla forces would merge into a single army.

Mandela announced the agreement to a televised press conference, speaking in three languages—English, Xhosa, and Afrikaans—to dramatize the new spirit of reconciliation.

"You are welcome in this country," he told whites who still threatened to resist. But he warned them that "democracy has no place for talk of civil war."

For those who yearned for democracy, the new constitution was a beautiful document. But it was still just a document. Now the people needed to choose leaders who could make it real. Because Mandela

Enthusiastic supporters at a Mandela rally in the Pampierstad Stadium in Bophuthatswana, April 9, 1994.

and de Klerk had spearheaded the development of the new constitution, it was only natural that both of them would campaign, among other candidates, to lead the newly liberated nation.

I have witnessed countless election campaigns in the United States and have written many articles on the process. Although the exercise of democracy always moves me, the political campaigns often feel phony. Candidates try to avoid controversial positions. Slick television ads take the place of real debate. Most voters don't even bother to show up and cast their ballot.

South Africa's first free election, by comparison, was thrilling. True, some candidates employed professional advisers, including a few from America, and there were television ads, photo ops, and slogans. ("Now is the time" was the ANC's catchphrase.) But it was mostly a spectacle of amateurs campaigning their hearts out.

Mandela, of course, was the main attraction. Following his caravan into the dusty black townships, I often felt that the entire frustrated history of black South Africa was exploding before my eyes. The motorcade would roll onto a barren soccer field surrounded by rickety bleachers, and the township would erupt in delirium. The throngs hung from lampposts and clung to the tops of fences. They filled the bleachers with a blaze of brightly colored sun umbrellas and climbed to the corrugated iron canopies, dancing to a rhythmic blast of African music and chanting, "Nelson Man-DEL-a! Nelson Man-DEL-a!"

On the campaign trail, candidate Nelson Mandela waves to the crowds in Bophuthatswana, April 9, 1994.

Mandela walked stiffly on chronically swollen feet. He wore a hearing aid. He was not the most exciting public speaker, and sometimes after a twelve-hour day of campaigning he was so tired that he would stumble over his words. It didn't matter. The fact that he was there was enough.

Perhaps the strangest sight was watching F. W. de Klerk and other white candidates from the National Party—the inventors of apartheid—campaign for black votes. Near bus stops, at farmers' markets, and once in a person's backyard in Soweto, the huge black township, I watched de Klerk putting on Zulu hats, watching traditional African dances, and shaking black hands.

At one campaign rally, where a crowd of five thousand blacks was lured by the promise of a free supper, de Klerk was introduced as a "strong chief" and the man "who liberated South Africa."

Then the candidate made his pitch: The National Party is entirely new. It ended apartheid. The African National Congress is a party of amateurs who will bring nothing but chaos. Everybody promises houses and jobs, but only the National Party has the business magic to deliver them.

People in the crowd with whom I spoke were doubtful, but there was something heartwarming about watching this white man—the head of a political party that, since 1948, had been devoted to the separation of the races—humble himself before the country's new voters.

"I'm white, but my heart pumps the same red blood as the red blood in the heart of every South African," de Klerk proclaimed.

President de Klerk shakes hands with schoolchildren at a campaign rally in Dwarsfontein; January 1994.

Throughout the campaign there was a frightening background noise of hate and violence. Township youths waved guns at campaign workers. Racial murder squads formed from radicals on both the white and black sides. There was an unspoken—but constant—worry that someone would try to assassinate one of the candidates.

Six weeks before voting day, thousands of armed white separatists converged on a black homeland called Bophuthatswana. The dictator of the homeland had appealed to them for help in preserving his little kingdom against the new democracy. The homeland soldiers and police, however, were turning against the tyrant. A few other journalists and I packed into a car and drove frantically to the impending showdown. We arrived in time to witness a horrifying scene. Three white farmers had been gunned down in a shootout with black men in Bophuthatswana police uniforms. One farmer was dead and the other two lay sprawled alongside their blue Mercedes, pleading for an ambulance. Suddenly one of the policemen stepped forward and executed the two men with four shots from his automatic rifle. Then he turned his gaze on us, as if wondering whether he should eliminate any witnesses. Luckily, he turned away. After further riots and fighting that took dozens of lives, President de Klerk ordered the homeland ruler deposed and order restored.

As the elections grew closer, the episodes of sabotage and terrorism increased. Explosions at black taxi terminals. A car bomb in downtown Johannesburg. A grenade tossed into a black restaurant. The government deployed one hundred thousand police officers and thousands of army reservists to protect polling places.

Members of the Afrikaner resistance plead for their lives during preelection violence in Bophuthatswana, March 1994.

The violence was clearly intended to frighten blacks away from the voting booths on the day of democracy. But it seemed to merely increase the eagerness for that day of liberation.

On April 27, 1994, I teamed up with a few other journalists and rented a small airplane for the election day that would end more than three hundred years of white rule. From early morning until twilight, we zoomed around the country, trying to observe this historical moment from as many angles as possible. We landed in Zululand, where we watched Mandela drop his ballot into a box before dozens of TV cameras—at age seventy-five, he was casting the first vote of his life. Then we flew to Mandela's boyhood home, Qunu, where villagers formed a patient line that zigzagged happily down the rocky hills and women brought picnics to the waiting voters. We flew to a picturesque old Afrikaner settlement and then to a corn-farming community where racists had recently bombed the ANC office. We spent the day talking to the country's new voters as they proudly lined up with nervous whites to decide who would run their future.

They came by the millions. Full citizens at last, they voted in mud schoolhouses under thorn trees, in urban ghetto clinics, and in

Villagers wait to vote in Bothaville, April 27, 1994.

blue tents pitched for the election in miserable shack towns. Although the ballots listed the names of the political parties that would make up the parliament, not individual leaders (parliament would later elect the president), they were voting for Nelson Mandela.

"As soon as we will have voted for him in power, then we will be free," said Jim Sandlana, sixty-seven, a retired gold miner in Qunu and one of the many new voters to whom I talked during our flying tour of the polls. After depositing his ballot, he announced, "My heart is relieved."

It is hard to describe the mix of emotions that washed over the country that day—the hearts full to bursting, the fears of what would come next. But at every stop, there was relief that South Africa had made it this far.

112

A few weeks later, I watched the new parliament convene in Cape Town, where the Dutch first settled. Traditionally the presiding officer had been a white man wearing a black frock coat, but on this day, the leader of the legislators was an Indian woman in a sari. Before her the assembly fanned out in a vivid display of races and costumes—white men in suits were outnumbered by black women in bright hats; former prisoners sat alongside their former jailers; returned exiles shared space with recycled racists; a Communist leader wearing red socks nodded to a white general heading a party of separatists. Everywhere were examples of whimsical reversal, none sweeter than that of Ahmed Kathrada, who had shared a Robben Island cellblock with Mandela. Today he was Mandela's designated minister of correctional services, responsible for overseeing the prison system.

Without a dissenting vote, the parliament chose Nelson Mandela to be president.

The men and women who would lead the new South Africa came from various backgrounds. Some of them had spent the apartheid years outside the country, trying to organize international protests. Thabo Mbeki, who would succeed Mandela as president,

114

was one of these exiles. Others had managed to find ways to challenge the system while staying within the law, such as Archbishop Desmond Tutu, who oversaw an Anglican archdiocese in Cape Town, and Cyril Ramaphosa, who represented the organization for black mine workers. But the core members of the new government had been groomed in prison—a place where they developed networks of friends, learned to outsmart the authorities, and also learned to negotiate.

Mandela often said his twenty-seven years in white men's prisons had not broken him or made him bitter but had trained him and his comrades for the hard work that still lay ahead.

"Whatever we knew, whatever we learned, we shared, and by sharing we multiplied whatever courage we had individually," he wrote. "Ultimately, we had to create our own lives in prison."

In 1997 Mandela paid tribute to their unusual education by emptying Robben Island of prisoners and turning it into a museum. Today it is one of the country's most popular tourist attractions.

Mandela's presidential inauguration followed a week after the parliament had convened. A crowd of world leaders, many of whom had shunned South Africa during the apartheid years, gathered on a government pavilion overlooking a joyous crowd of fifty thousand people on a wide lawn below.

They sang not one national anthem but two: "Die Stem van Suid-Afrika" ("The Call of South Africa"), the official Afrikaans anthem, and "Nkosi Sikelel' iAfrika" ("God Bless Africa"), a liberation anthem, which turned the crowd on the lawn into an immense choir. They raised the new national flag, another bright compromise—it contained the black,

South African Army helicopters fly the national flag during the Inauguration ceremonies in Pretoria, May 10, 1994.

green, and yellow that was popular with liberation organizations and the red, white, and blue that the whites had imported from the British and Dutch flags.

With the commanding dignity that had carried him through more than half a century of defiance, captivity, and reconciliation, Nelson Rolihlahla Mandela swore the oath of office and became the first black president of South Africa.

The aging leader opened his five-year term with a gentle speech about shared patriotism, addressing South Africans' common love of the soil, their common pain for their country's humiliation, and their common relief at finally being part of the civilized world.

"Never, never, and never again shall it be that this beautiful land will again experience the oppression of one by another and suffer the indignity of being the skunk of the world," he said.

The new president, now also the commander in chief of the armed forces, reviewed lines of South African troops, a military that was created in large part to prevent someone like him from taking power. Nine jet fighters of the South African air force streaked overhead as part of an aerial salute, and the citizens assembled on the grass sent up a roar. Then the new president took the old president, F. W. de Klerk, by the arm and led him down to meet the crowd.

Four years and three months earlier, Mandela was serving a life sentence for trying to overthrow the government. Today he led it.

A South African soldier enjoys his crowd control duty at Nelson Mandela's Inauguration in Pretoria, May 10, 1994.

Thabo Mbeki shakes hands with F. W. de Klerk while the newly elected President Mandela looks on; Pretoria, May 1994. Mbeki served as Mandela's vice president.

Nelson Mandela settled in to a seat on his presidential jet. He propped his swollen feet up on two pillows and accepted a bowl of cereal and a plate of fruit from an attendant.

CHAPTER 6

PRESIDENT MANDELA

It was six a.m. on his 122nd day in office, and he had agreed to let me and a South African reporter tag along for the day while he did his job.

As we flew to Cape Town, where the South African parliament meets, we chatted about a speech he had given the night before to a group of trade union leaders. Mandela was still working every day to calm the fears of whites and to persuade white-owned businesses to invest more money, produce more jobs, and help lift the poorest out of their misery. At the same time, Mandela was working just as hard to keep his devoted supporters from losing patience.

Poking at his fruit, Mandela recalled the scolding he had delivered to his union friends, who were eager to start flexing their muscles, demanding better pay and benefits.

Wait, Mandela had warned the union leaders. *Hold off on the strikes and protests. You are scaring foreign investors. I understand that your workers want better pay, but think about the five million people who have no jobs at all. Prepare to tighten your belts and accept low wages, so that foreign companies will build more factories and generate more jobs. That is how some Asian countries became economic tigers.*

In his cabinet, parliament, and the provincial governments, the new president had a strong supporting cast made up of former prisoners, former exiles, and men and women who had become leaders during the years of opposition. But probably none of them had the personal stature to say what Mandela had stated the night before to the unionists and to expect the respectful hearing he received.

At 7:50 a.m. on August 4, 1994, his plane landed at an air force base outside Cape Town and the day officially began.

The office Mandela inherited from the past president contained few personal touches. I recognized a photo of the village where he grew up and pictures of two young boxers sparring in Soweto in 1957—one of them clearly the young Nelson Mandela. But there was not much else representing his amazing life.

The vibe, however, was pure Mandela. The staff around him included men and women of all races, and Mandela insisted everyone be treated with courtesy. Each visitor, including cabinet ministers and foreign ambassadors, was invited to shake hands with the woman who served the tea. Although today Mandela wore a gray three-piece suit and tie for meetings with foreign diplomats, he usually preferred

The 1957 photograph of Nelson Mandela sparring with a friend.

to come to work in a colorful, custom-tailored African shirt.

Mandela's reputation—and his country's successful transition—had radiated hope beyond his nation, and part of his day was spent meeting officials from neighboring countries that were suffering from war or political conflict. They came to the new South African president hoping his magic could help settle their own country's problems.

Mandela's fame also drew visitors from around the globe, eager to pose for pictures with the great man. His secretary told me he received two hundred such requests every day. He turned down most of them, she said, but he could never resist children or people who would bring money to South Africa.

"Well, it's a real pleasure to meet you, and we appreciate the aid," Mandela said, shaking hands with a smiling delegation of Japanese businessmen.

Most of his day was spent in the shepherd's role, gently urging his country to stick together and move forward. His government was a fragile coalition made up of vastly different political factions, including his comrades from the struggle against apartheid, representatives of the white National Party, and members of the Inkatha Freedom Party, the contentious Zulu group. Part of Mandela's job was to prevent small tensions from growing into serious disputes.

President Nelson Mandela shakes hands with Microsoft chairman Bill Gates at a global health conference in Seattle; December 1999.

On this day, for example, Mandela was trying to decide whether he should accept an invitation from the Zulu king to attend a big celebration honoring the great warrior Shaka. Mandela's main Zulu political rival, Mangosuthu Buthelezi, who was now part of the government, did not want Mandela stealing the spotlight at the Shaka Day celebration. This was no small matter—before the election, fighting between Mandela's loyalists and Buthelezi's followers had killed thousands of people. The threat of violence still lingered.

The president spent a portion of his day surveying the problems besetting his government. He had a meeting to discuss getting more money in the budget for the police force, which was battling rising crime. He conferred with the head of parliament about demands for more government spending on housing for the country's millions of shack-dwellers. He talked with health officials about screening for the virus that causes AIDS—an epidemic crisis in southern Africa. He worried whether the vast, mostly white civil service he inherited would be loyal to the new democratic leadership.

Late in the day President Mandela's chief legal adviser came by with documents to sign. Some of them were letters to retiring officials of the state

Nelson Mandela at an AIDS benefit concert, March 2005.

6664

intelligence service, thanking them for their years of work. Mandela shook his head in mild amazement. Not so long ago, one of the main jobs of the intelligence service had been to attack opposition leaders like Mandela. Here he was, signing thank-you letters for people who might have tried to kill him.

"This might be a fellow who was putting bombs in installations and injuring innocent people," Mandela said, holding up one of the letters. He shook his head again and signed it.

My day with President Mandela ended as he went off to dinner with some African diplomats. What was clear from watching him at work was how heavily the country depended on Mandela's personal charm and the awe he inspired. I wondered—everybody wondered—would that be enough?

When Mandela reached the first anniversary of his presidency— and just before I left South Africa for a new assignment as an editor in New York—I made a farewell tour of the country, visiting cities, disbanded homelands, and black townships, hoping to take a measure of how the country was doing.

One place that seemed to offer hope was Port Elizabeth, which had long been the center of South Africa's car-making industry. Since Mandela's election, Port Elizabeth had become the first white city to elect a black mayor and the first to begin diverting money from affluent white neighborhoods in order to start improving life in its wretched black township.

Soweto-on-Sea, the neighborhood where most of Port Elizabeth's black population lived, was still a miserable slum, located alongside an estuary polluted by sewage. Pink flamingos flapped overhead. A bitter wind sliced through huts made of scrap tin and pasteboard. But there were signs that Soweto-on-Sea was getting some attention. Whereas a year earlier a single slop bucket had served as the toilet for half a dozen families, now Soweto-on-Sea was dotted with concrete outhouses connected to sewers. High-masted streetlights had been erected to illuminate the alleys where criminals lurked, and electricity was coming to many shanties. On a hillside a few miles away, bulldozers were grooming plots of land so that families now jammed into shacks in others' backyards could at least have land of their own. There were two busy new playgrounds, and a site had been selected for a new school. The older schools offered children a daily snack of peanut butter sandwiches and fruit juice under President Mandela's school nutrition program.

Whenever I stopped a resident of Soweto-on-Sea to ask if life was better, however, the instinctive first reaction was almost always the same: No, not really. What about jobs? What about real houses instead of shacks?

"We struggled before the election," said Lucy Maquma, who was peddling shoes from a rickety wooden stand at a bus stop. "We are still struggling even now."

And for every place like Soweto-on-Sea, there were many places in South Africa unreached by change or where change had been wrestled to a standstill by the defenders of the traditional order.

Villagers collect water at a communal tap in a squatter settlement in Soweto; August 2002.

When Mandela took office, the big question was whether the African National Congress could transform itself from a liberation movement into a government.

The answer was now pretty clear—yes, and despite some fumbles and a few scandals, it was a government that inspired respect among whites and pride among blacks.

It was true that in its first year Mandela's government had delivered fewer than one thousand of the million houses it had promised to build in its first five-year term. There was, so far, little relief for neglected black schools and no measurable improvement in the unemployment rate—41 percent of blacks still had no real jobs.

But Mandela's team had delivered a stable peace, a steadily growing economy, and a gradual transformation of institutions that had served the old order. Not long before, the military had been the blunt instrument of apartheid. Now the South African Defense Force was racially integrated and the defense minister was a former antiapartheid guerrilla. The police, more deeply implicated in the cruelties of the old system, were slower to change. The police force was still divided by racial tensions, officers were impatient about low pay, and the crime rate was high. But at least the police were beginning to see their job as protecting all of South Africa's people, not just the whites.

116

The Truth and Reconciliation Commission, created in 1995, promised people would not suffer any punishment if they confessed fully to crimes they had committed during apartheid. Some South Africans were bitterly angry that leaders of the apartheid regime—and some outright killers—were allowed to go free after testifying. But the process allowed many families to learn the fate of loved ones who had disappeared under apartheid and is widely credited with helping the country move on. Other divided countries in Africa, Latin America, and elsewhere have imitated South Africa's example.

South Africa, after one year of democracy, looked and felt like another country. Black newscasters read the evening news, classrooms in once-white schools were filled with children of all ethnicities, black townships cheered the police they used to fear, and sporting events mixed races. The black middle class was growing and influential (most of the new government belonged to it). Best of all was the drastic decline in murderous political violence.

But for the poorest South Africans, the political changes were already old news. The real test now was how they lived, and on that subject people were getting cranky. Toilets and peanut butter sandwiches might be progress, but they did not feel like victory. And millions were still waiting, even for those "luxuries." The slow pace of tangible improvements—especially houses, which had become the main symbol of success or failure in a country with eight million homeless people—was disheartening.

A mother in Soweto boils water using a kerosene stove.

Still, there was little bitterness or despair, because few South African blacks had expected overnight magic. They recognized that even if the circumstances of daily life had not changed all that much, at least the direction had.

"The old government didn't care about us," said Makhosi Khanyile, a mother I met on a muddy slope in a Zulu slum north of Durban, a city I visited on my farewell tour. "People feel that this government is theirs. They are still waiting for the promises, it is true, but if sometimes they get angry with this government, that is their right, because it is theirs."

Mandela finished his five-year term as president with the spirit of reconciliation still mostly intact. On a continent where men have traditionally spilled blood to hold on to power, just the fact that Mandela stepped down after his allotted years was a rare act of statesmanship. In 1999, he was succeeded by Thabo Mbeki, the son of another Robben Island prisoner. Mandela settled into a busy retirement with his third wife, Graca Machel, whom he married on his eightieth birthday (he and the rabble-rousing Winnie divorced in 1996). He still worked tirelessly, promoting AIDS awareness and other causes.

Under President Mbeki, crime and corruption increased, the scourge of AIDS worsened, and millions remained without jobs or decent homes. The population of blacks living in misery increased due to refugees escaping to South Africa from neighboring countries like Zimbabwe, where Robert Mugabe had brought persecution and financial ruin. Many whites left South Africa for England, Australia, or the United States. Compared to the rest of Africa, much of it ravaged by war, disease, and the most abject poverty, South Africa was still a land of stability and promise. But the promise remained out of reach for many.

The question that has hovered urgently over South Africa since the birth of its democracy—can the nation narrow the gap between rich and poor and offer its majority the hope of prosperity along with the gift of freedom?—remains unanswered. Thanks to Mandela's legacy, though, the answer is in the hands of all South Africans today.

Soweto, February 1990.

In June 2007, I took my daughter Molly to South Africa. I had an invitation to speak at a conference of journalists in Cape Town, and decided to use this opportunity to introduce my curious fifth grader to a place I love.

LOOKING BACK

We drove down the coast to see the colony of African penguins at Boulders. We took the tram up Table Mountain. We spent an afternoon in the sprawling shack town of Khayelitsha, at a clinic for women infected with the HIV virus. I even dragged Molly to a speech by Mandela's successor, President Thabo Mbeki, who had disappointed many of his countrymen as an uninspiring leader.

The country I showed my daughter still had lingering racial resentments, still had a vast gap between rich and poor, still suffered from a high level of violent crime. It was also still breathtakingly beautiful, and still a vibrant, if unfinished, democracy.

After a few days, we flew to Johannesburg for the highlight of our trip—a meeting with Nelson Mandela.

I had not seen him in a dozen years. Mandela had long ago stopped giving interviews to journalists. His hearing and memory were fading, and his loyal staff fended off reporters for fear that he might say something controversial or embarrassing. They agreed to let me see him and ask a few questions. Not an interview, exactly. Just a conversation. For old time's sake.

Molly was about to turn ten. Mandela was about to turn eighty-nine. His knees stiff with arthritis, he stayed seated behind his desk, but he beamed a great smile and shook Molly's hand and asked her name.

"Marley?" he repeated.

"Molly," we corrected.

"And what do you want to be when you grow up?"

"Maybe a writer," she said.

"A waiter? Well, ah, that is interesting . . ."

Time was short. I plunged ahead with the question that everyone always asks about Nelson Mandela: After all you went through, friends tortured and killed, decades in prison, your family tormented, your people humiliated, how can you not feel hatred and bitterness?

Mandela sighed patiently, as if the question was silly. To a leader, he said, hatred is just a distraction. It keeps you from thinking clearly. He talked about the angry young radicals who spent time with him in the prison on Robben Island. They were always in a rage, always talking about waging war against the white oppressors.

"What are you going to do?" Mandela would ask them.

"We will attack and destroy them!"

"All right, have you analyzed how strong they are, the enemy? Have you compared their strength to your strength?"

"No, we will just attack!"

Foolish young men, blind with hate.

Of course Nelson Mandela felt what other men feel, but he usually mastered his feelings. He was, at heart, the most practical of men. He always asked himself, *What will work?* If that meant making deals with people he did not like or respect, he would do it. If it meant giving something up in the short run to achieve success in the long run, he would do it. Compromise is often the hardest, bravest course. It requires standing up to your enemies, and sometimes it means standing up to your friends.

Mandela would be the first to say he was not a saint. He was a disobedient youth, a neglectful husband, and a distracted father. He sometimes misled his allies and manipulated his followers. He was willing to let innocent people die in the cause of liberation. He befriended some terrible despots from other countries and kept quiet about their cruelties because they supported the South African struggle.

He had principles, of course, but he would often bend them to get what he wanted—which, for most of his life, was the right of Africans to govern themselves. As a leader, he was, at different points in his career, a militant and a moderate, a tyrant and a servant of the people, a champion of the downtrodden and a friend of big business. Time and again, he let the end justify the means.

He preferred common sense to sentiment. The vacation home he built in his boyhood village after being released from prison was an almost exact replica of the warden's cottage where he had lived at the end of his imprisonment. An interviewer asked him what on earth had inspired him to copy his jailer's house. Was it a fondness for his prison experience? Was it a gesture of forgiveness? Nothing of the kind, Mandela replied. He had simply gotten used to the warden's floor plan. He wanted to build himself a house where he could find the bathroom at night without stumbling in the dark.

If he was not a messiah, he was not merely a revolutionary, either, because revolutionaries tend to think they have finished their job once they have torn down the old order. He was, rather, a shrewd balancer of honor and interests, of principles and goals. He was a politician.

Politician is not a word that commands great respect these days. This is, perhaps, because so few politicians are like Nelson Mandela. He combined a high purpose, an unusually clear vision of his ultimate destination, an irresistible charm, and seemingly bottomless reserves of patience, self-discipline, and resourcefulness.

He gave millions of South Africans a peaceful, if imperfect, young democracy that few imagined possible. And he gave history a model of leadership few on any continent have matched. And finally, unlike so many men who fall in love with power, when his time was up he stepped aside.

When our visit was nearly over, I asked Mandela about the future of South Africa. He started to give the polite answer, the optimistic answer, but then he paused and changed direction: "We have a leader, however, President Thabo Mbeki, who is trying to depart from our experience . . ." In a stern voice, he complained that Mbeki liked to give orders without listening to the people around him. That was not what South Africa needed.

Out of the corner of my eye, I saw a panicky look on the face of Mandela's assistant. What if word of this got out? This was going to be a scandal!

Mandela smiled broadly. Just a last bit of mischief from the Tree Shaker.

Articles

10

In 1964, an editorial in The New York Times *compared Nelson Mandela and the other members of the African National Congress who were convicted of conspiracy to the Founding Fathers of the United States.*

VERDICT IN SOUTH AFRICA
June 14, 1964

A worldwide campaign of protest has already begun against the life sentence imposed by South Africa's Supreme Court on African Nationalist leader Nelson R. Mandela and seven other foes of apartheid. As the debate and votes in the United Nations this past year have shown, most of the world regards the convicted men as heroes and freedom fighters. They are considered the George Washingtons and Benjamin Franklins of South Africa, not criminals deserving punishment.

In the wake of these sentences, the pressure for a complete trade boycott of South Africa and for its expulsion from the United Nations will increase. And continuance of South Africa's indefensible policies makes it increasingly difficult for the United States and others to resist this pressure.

The protests being heard now are, of course, only incidentally directed at the sentences. Basically, they reflect the outraged conscience of the world; they mirror the growing moral disgust among men of every color at the rigid racism of the South African government, at its denial of political rights for the majority of South Africa's inhabitants and at its readiness to use violence to repress the black African.

By steadily choking off every hope for peaceful change, the South African Government has encouraged the black majority of its subjects to turn their thoughts toward violence as the only means of breaking the fetters that bind them. There is tragedy in the fact that Mr. Mandela and others of those convicted with him began their political careers seeking, in the words he employed in his eloquent speech last April, "to achieve a non-racial State by non-violence" and then felt themselves driven toward violence by the South African Government itself.

If disaster is to be averted in South Africa, those who now hold the reins of power there must re-examine the policies that are sowing the seeds of holocaust. Only a turn toward democracy and conciliation of the races can hold out hope for a happy future in that troubled land.

21

The discovery of diamonds and gold in South Africa led to a rush to mine the land and spawned worldwide tales of riches. This article tells how the diamonds were found. Many variations of this story were told, and it's difficult to say how much of it is true. "Kafir" was a derogatory term used by the white settlers to refer to native tribesmen.

HOW DIAMONDS WERE FOUND IN SOUTH AFRICA
July 28, 1878

The modern discovery of diamonds came about this wise: in 1867, a certain John O'Reilly, trader and hunter, on his way from the interior, reached the junction of the rivers, and stopped for the night at the farm of a Dutch farmer named Van Niekerk. The children were playing on the earth floor with some pretty pebbles they had found long before in the river. One of these pebbles attracted O'Reilly's attention. He said, picking it up, "That might be a diamond." Niekerk laughed, and said he could have it; it was no diamond; if it was, there were plenty around there. However, O'Reilly was not to be launched out of his idea, and said that if Niekerk didn't object he would take it down with him to Cape Town and see what it was, and if it proved to be of value, he would give him half the proceeds. On the way down, a long journey, he stopped at Colesburg, at the hotel, and showed the pebble, scratching with it a pane of glass. His friends laughingly scratched glass with a gunflint, and threw the pebble out of the window, telling O'Reilly not to make a fool of himself. However, Reilly persevered, got it to Dr. Atherstone, near the coast, who announced that it was in truth a diamond of $22^{1}/_{2}$ carats. It was sold for $3,000. I am glad to say that O'Reilly divided fairly with Niekirk. The latter remembered that he had seen an immense stone in the hands of a Kafir witch doctor, who used it in his

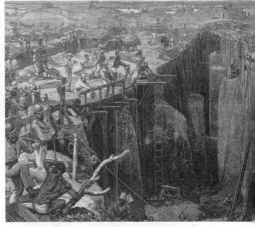
Etching of a South African diamond mine, 1872.

incantations. He found the fetish man, gave him 500 sheep, horses, and nearly all he possessed, and sold it the same day to an experienced diamond buyer for $56,000. This was the famous "Star of South Africa." It weighed $83^{1}/_{2}$ carats in the rough, and was found to be a gem quite the rival of any Indian stone in purity and brilliance. After it had been cut it was bought by the Earl of Dudley, and it is now known as the "Dudley" diamond.

The native crawled over the ground and found many more, and the excitement grew and became intense. By 1869 parties in ox-wagons had worked their way over the weary plains to the Vaal River. From all parts of the colony and from foreign lands people swarmed, and soon, like the creation of a dream, a tented city of 12,000 and more grew at Pniel and Kipdrift, the opposite banks of the stream, where diamonds were found plentifully and of excellent quality by sorting over the bolder-drift. Soon, hundreds of cradles, like those used by the Australian gold-diggers, were rocking on the edge of the stream, supplied with the previous gravel by a large force of diggers, sievers, and carriers. People were thunderstruck at their success. The excited crowds shifted their quarters up and down the river, making new discoveries during 1870 and 1871, over an area of from 40 to 50 miles of the stream.

23

Mohandas Gandhi, whose ideas about nonviolent protest inspired civil rights activists around the world, began his campaign for the rights of Indians in South Africa. This article, written on his death, reflects the reverence that was felt for Gandhi and highlights his history in Africa.

MILLIONS ESTEEMED GANDHI AS A SAINT
January 31, 1948

Mohandas Karamchand Gandhi, Hindu reformer and nationalist leader, was looked upon as a saint by millions of his followers, who bestowed upon him the admiring appellation of "Mahatma," literally "the great-souled one."

He was born on Oct. 2, 1869, at Porbander, on the Kathiawar peninsula of India, and came of a Bania family with official traditions. His father had been Prime Minister of the little native state.

At the age of 19 Gandhi went to London, where he studied at University College and was called to the bar by the Inner Temple.

Returning to India Gandhi practiced law for a short time in the Bombay High Court, but in 1893 he was called to South Africa on professional business. There he became engrossed in a long struggle for the liberties of Indians who had migrated to that country, which was his principal occupation for more than twenty years. Both in Natal and the

Gandhi and his associates pose in front of his law offices in South Africa, ca. 1895.

Transvaal race feeling against the Indian settlers was strong and discriminations were many.

When, in 1896, after a brief visit to India, Gandhi returned to Durban, he was attacked and badly beaten for his agitations. The South Africans had become incensed at a pamphlet he wrote in India on the conditions of the Indian in South Africa. It was then that his conception of passive nonviolent resistance developed. He relinquished his large income as a lawyer and founded a colony, the Tolstoy Farm, near Durban.

He was often imprisoned and more often subjected to indignities, but this neither checked his energies nor deterred him from rendering service of marked loyalty to the British Government.

In 1914, soon after a commission had removed some of the worst sources of injustice to the Indians living in South Africa, Gandhi returned to his native land and threw himself into support of the home rule movement. By 1918 he was busy organizing his Satyagraha (literally "Insistence upon truth") movement, which he defined as follows:

"Satyagraha differs from passive resistance as the North Pole from the South. The latter has been conceived as a weapon for the weak and does not exclude the use of physical force or violence for the purpose of gaining one's end, whereas the former has been conceived as a weapon of the strongest and excludes the use of violence in any shape or form."

32

As Mandela's fame grew during his imprisonment, his first family lived outside of the limelight. In 1989, a New York Times *reporter visited family members to find out what they thought of their famous father. Only Mandela's daughter Makaziwe is alive today.*

MANDELA LIVES WITHOUT REGRETS, HIS SON REPORTS
By Christopher S. Wren
Cofimvaba, South Africa, December 19, 1989

In this dusty farm town lost among the rolling green hills of the Transkei homeland, a shopkeeper awaits the release of a father who has passed 10,000 days in captivity.

The father is Nelson Mandela, probably the world's most famous political prisoner. The shopkeeper, Makgatho L. Mandela, is his only surviving son and has visited him twice this month at the Victor Verster Prison outside Cape Town.

While the world has accorded Nelson Mandela's second wife, Winnie, who is 55 years old, and their two daughters celebrity status, his first wife, Evelyn Ntoko, a 69-year-old retired nurse, lives quietly in this rural community of Xhosa villagers.

Two of Mr. Mandela's four children from his first marriage have died, leaving Makgatho and his younger sister, Makaziwe, who is studying for a doctorate in social anthropology at the University of Massachusetts. They were born in Soweto, the sprawling black township outside Johannesburg.

Makgatho was only 12 years old and a schoolboy in Swaziland when his father was put in jail in 1962.

"It was difficult at the first years," said Makgatho Mandela, who is now 39. "I yearned for him." He tried to write his father, he said, though the prison authorities restricted his letters to family matters.

He was allowed to start visiting his father in June 1967, first at Robben Island, South Africa's equivalent of Alcatraz, and then after 1982 at Pollsmoor Prison in Cape Town.

Nelson Mandela nearly died of tuberculosis in August 1986, prompting the South African authorities to move him to a more comfortable warden's house on a prison farm at Paarl outside Cape Town, where Makgathok last saw him on Dec. 10 and 12. "When I visited him on the island, we had only one visit every six months," Makgatho Mandela said. Now, he said, he can pick up the telephone and arrange an appointment through the prison guards.

During their prison visits, Makgatho Mandela and his father usually discuss the family, he said. They are arranging to rebuild the ruined family homestead at Nelson Mandela's birthplace of Qunu, near Umtata. Makgato Mandela said his father would come for family gatherings and reunions but would not stay there.

Nelson Mandela, he said, wanted to return to the simple brick house where he once lived in Soweto. He would not move into the more lavish mansion that Winnie Mandela built earlier for his return.

The son said his father displayed no bitterness in his 28th year of confinement. "He feels he has been on the right track all along," Makgatho Mandela said.

"His whole purpose in life is the struggle for a free, democratic united South Africa. So he does not regret anything."

42

In the immediate aftermath of the Sharpeville Massacre, officials estimated that seventy-two protesters had been killed. Later, that number was changed to sixty-nine. An article published after the massacre captures the indignation overseas as well as the increasing tension in South Africa.

SOUTH AFRICA: RISING RACIAL TENSIONS
By Leonard Ingalls
Johannesburg, South Africa, March 26, 1960

The tragedy of South Africa appeared this week to be moving ever faster toward an ugly climax. The police shooting of more than 250 African political demonstrators—seventy-two of them fatally, by official count—has drawn racial tension to a critical point. The country is still in a state of shock over the grim events; the question in many minds is what must be done to change the sad and hopeless course upon which South Africa finds itself.

There is a growing realization among South Africans that their country is out of step in its racial policies, not only with the rest of sub-Sahara Africa but with the rest of the world. This feeling received considerable stimulus from a speech last month in Capetown by Prime Minister Macmillan warning that a "wind of change" was blowing through this continent.

Nevertheless, the Nationalist Party Government headed by Prime Minister Hendrik F. Verwoerd has thus far shown little disposition to make any basic change in its policy of segregation.

The root of the problem is in numbers. There are 3,000,000 whites and about 11,500,000 persons whose skins are black or brown. Nearly 10,000,000 of these are Africans. The whites, fearful they will be "overwhelmed," are afraid to grant the Africans full political rights and freedom of movement.

The bodies of the dead and wounded lie in the street after police opened fire on protesters in Sharpeville; March 21, 1960.

Two Party Backing

Out of this fear has grown the policy of white supremacy that, in its basic form, is supported both by the governing Nationalist Party and by its principal rival, the United Party.

In the last few years, under the guidance of Dr. Verwoerd, first as Minister of Native (African) Affairs and more recently as Prime Minister, the Nationalists have devised the program of apartheid, or separate development. They say it means that Africans may govern themselves and live as freely as they wish in areas set aside for them by the whites.

No provision is made for African representation in the South African Parliament. When Africans are permitted to enter white areas, as they must to provide the inexpensive labor upon which the economy is based, they will be subject to the same old color bar, second-class status and indignities in deference to white supremacy they have always faced.

The gains of African nationalism to the north and those that are soon to come have hardened many white South Africans in their view that nothing of the kind shall occur here. Others who are critics of Prime Minister Verwoerd and his followers are seeking a compromise. The Africans are becoming more determined to settle for nothing less than their cousins elsewhere.

300-Year History

An indication of the fact that the Government is prepared to use its defense forces to quell ruthlessly any African uprising was given this week when jet aircraft swooped over the demonstrators in an effort to discourage them. There is little doubt that the jets would open fire if there were a mass rebellion.

Ranged against the highly organized whites is the African mass, lacking in military training, poorly educated, loosely organized and ill-prepared except by passion and pure weight of numbers to win anything by physical force. Yet during the last year in many parts of South Africa Africans have engaged in demonstrations against their plight that have cost some of them their lives.

The major African political organization is the African National Congress; led by Chief Albert Luthuli, a patient, mature, and intelligent man. Congress, as it is known, has existed for nearly fifty years and has waged many campaigns to direct attention to African grievances.

The government has recognized the value of the organization as a sort of safety valve, but whenever it becomes too loud and its leaders too bold, the authorities move in to arrest the leaders, ban meetings, disperse demonstrators, confine Chief Luthuli to his home and place some member on trial for treason.

In April of last year some younger members broke away to form the Pan-Africanist Congress as a more militant political organization. Two of their chief goals, to be achieved, they said, by 1963, are a free African trade union and votes for all.

Their first major demonstration was against passes, the hated papers all Africans are required to carry under national laws governing their movements, employment, and status as citizens. The African National Congress also has campaigned against passes for many years, but to no avail.

Passive Resistance

The Africanists decided to dispose arbitrarily of their passes and to offer themselves for arrest in a mass. It was during their demonstrations in African dwelling areas near Johannesburg and Capetown that the police fired.

As a result of subsequent actions banning meetings and advancing legislation to outlaw African political organizations, the future of African political activity is in doubt. In spite of growing uncertainty among many white South Africans Prime Minister Verwoerd and his Government seem determined to insist on denying the African any national voice.

A Test of Strength

Thus the situation is a test of strength for Dr. Verwoerd.

The suppression of African nationalism has led to bloodshed many times in South Africa and it is not likely that the course being followed will have any less violent result in the future. Some observers believe that the Verwoerd Administration cannot survive a repetition of this week's tragic events and that the Nationalist Party itself would seek a Prime Minister with a more moderate policy if they recurred.

Possibly the biggest question of all is what the Africans will do next. They have been bitter and resentful for a long time because they are not treated with ordinary human consideration. The slaying of their fellows has appalled them.

Under the conditions prevailing there does not seem to be much they can do but demonstrate and run the risk of being shot at. They are patient people and time certainly is on their side. South Africa may become the last outpost of white domination in Africa, but with world sentiment for the Africans here growing and sub-Sahara Africa gradually coming under African rule, there seems little doubt that the Africans in South Africa will one day have at least an equal share in their country's affairs.

In the years following the Rivonia Trial, Nelson Mandela's statements to the court were suppressed. In 1990, The New York Times *ran this article highlighting his speech. A recording of the speech, made public in 2001, has slightly different wording. One example is in the concluding paragraph—see page 44 for the definitive version.*

WHAT MANDELA WANTS: STATEMENTS AT HIS '64 TRIAL
February 11, 1990

The South African authorities have announced that Nelson Mandela will be freed today, giving him the opportunity to make his first statement in a public place in more than twenty-five years. His last such statement, on April 20, 1964, came from the dock at the Rivonia Trial.

Following are excerpts from his Rivonia speech, which remains his most thorough public account of his political beliefs.

"My Humble Contribution"

At the outset, I want to say that the suggestion made by the state in its opening that the struggle in South Africa is under the influence of foreigners or Communists is wholly incorrect. I have done whatever I did, both as an individual and as a leader of my people, because of my experience in South Africa and my own proudly felt African background, and not because of what any outsider might have said.

In my youth in the Transkei I listened to the elders of my tribe. Amongst the tales they related were those of wars fought by our ancestors in defense of the fatherland. . . . I hoped then that life might offer me the opportunity to serve my people and make my own humble contribution to their freedom struggle. . . .

Resorting to Violence

We felt that without violence there would be no way open to the African people to succeed in their struggle against the principle of white supremacy. All lawful modes of expressing opposition to this principle had been closed by the legislation, and we were placed in a position in which we had to either accept a permanent state of inferiority or to defy the Government. . . . We first broke the law in a way which avoided any recourse to violence; when this form was legislated against, and when the Government resorted to a show of force to crush opposition to its policies, only then did we decide to answer violence with violence.

But the violence we chose to adopt was not terrorism. We who formed Umkonto were all members of the African National Congress, and had behind us the A.N.C. tradition of nonviolence and negotiations as a means of solving political disputes. We believed that South Africa belonged to all the people who lived in it, and not to one group, be it black or white. We did not want an interracial war, and tried to avoid it to the last minute. . . .

This then was the plan: Umkonto was to perform sabotage, and strict instructions were given to its members, right from the start, that on no account were they to injure or kill people in planning or carrying out operations. . . .

An Ideal Political System

I have denied that I am a Communist, and I think that in the circumstances I am obliged to state exactly what my political beliefs are. I have always regarded myself . . . as an African patriot. . . .

Mandela speaks in 1961.

Today, I am attracted by the idea of a classless society, an attraction which springs in part from Marxist reading and in part from my admiration of the structure and organization of early African societies in this country. The land, then the main means of production, belonged to the tribe. There were no rich or poor and there was no exploitation. . . .

From my reading of Marxist literature and from conversations with Marxists, I have gained the impression that Communists regard the parliamentary system of the West as undemocratic and reactionary. But on the contrary, I am an admirer of such a system.

Magna Carta, the Petition of Rights and the Bill of Rights are documents held in veneration by democrats throughout the world. I have great respect for British political institutions, and for the country's system of justice. I regard the British Parliament as the most democratic institution in the world, and the independence and impartiality of its judiciary never fail to arouse my admiration.

The American Congress, that country's doctrine of separation of powers, as well as the independence of its judiciary, arouse in me similar sentiments.

I have been influenced in my thinking by both West and East. All this has led me to feel that in my search for a political formula, I should be absolutely impartial and objective. I should tie myself to no particular system of society other than that of socialism. I must leave myself free to borrow the best from the West and from the East. . . .

A Lack of Dignity

The Government often answers its critics by saying that Africans in South Africa are economically better off than the inhabitants of the other countries in Africa. I do not know whether this statement is true and doubt whether any comparison can be made without having regard to the cost-of-living index in such countries.

But even if it is true, as far as the African people are concerned it is irrelevant. Our complaint is not that we are poor by comparison with people in other countries, but that we are poor by comparison with the white people in our own country, and that we are prevented by legislation from altering this imbalance.

The lack of human dignity experienced by Africans is the direct result of the policy of white supremacy. White supremacy implies black inferiority. Legislation designed to preserve white supremacy entrenches this notion.

Menial tasks in South Africa are invariably performed by Africans. When anything has to be carried or cleaned the white man will look around for an African to do it for him, whether the African is employed by him or not.

Because of this sort of attitude, whites tend to regard Africans as a separate breed. They do not look upon them as people with families of their own; they do not realize that they have emotions, that they fall in love like white people do, that they want to be with their wives and children like white people want to be with theirs, that they want to earn enough money to support their families properly, to feed and clothe them and send them to school. . . .

What Africans Want

Africans want to be paid a living wage. Africans want to perform work they are capable of doing, and not work the Government declares them to be capable of. Africans want to be allowed to live where they obtain work, and not be endorsed out of an area because they were not born there.

Africans want to be allowed to own land in places where they work, and not be obliged to live in rented houses they can never call their own. Africans want to be part of the general population, and not confined to living in their own ghettos. . . .

Above all, we want equal political rights, because without them our disabilities will be permanent. I know this sounds revolutionary to the whites in this country, because the majority of voters will be Africans. This makes the white man fear democracy.

But this fear cannot be allowed to stand in the way of the only solution which will guarantee racial harmony and freedom for all. It is not true that the enfranchisement of all will result in racial domination. Political division, based on color, is entirely artificial, and when it disappears, so will the domination of one color group by another. The A.N.C. has spent half a century fighting against racialism. When it triumphs it will not change that policy.

This then is what A.N.C. is fighting. Their struggle is a truly national one. It is a struggle of the African people, inspired by their own suffering and their own experience. It is a struggle for the right to live.

During my lifetime I have dedicated myself to this struggle of the African people. I have fought against white domination, and I have fought against black domination. I have cherished the ideal of a democratic and free society in which all persons live together in harmony and with equal opportunities. It is an ideal I hope to live for and to achieve. But if needs be, it is an ideal for which I am prepared to die.

52

Although Mandela was officially banned from communicating with the outside world, his popularity grew during his prison term.

MANDELA, 70, CAPTIVATES EVEN THOSE WHO JAIL HIM
By John D. Battersby
Johannesburg, South Africa, July 17, 1988

After more than quarter of a century behind prison bars, Nelson Rolihlahla Mandela, a legend in his own lifetime, is sometimes portrayed as holding the Pretoria Government captive.

"The more pressure there is to release a person, the more difficult it becomes to release him," said Information Minister Stoffel J. Van der Merwe. "Then one becomes a hostage. If you concede to one person, then you invite pressure from all sides for the next thing."

Mr. Mandela's release has become a symbol of progress toward ending the apartheid system.

A Tightening Net

Enmeshed in a tightening net of black resistance, regional hostility and international sanctions, Pretoria has found it impossible to gain the cooperation even of conservative blacks while Mr. Mandela is in jail.

Mr. Mandela turns 70 on Monday, and he was to have received a six-hour visit from his wife, Winnie Nomzamo Mandela, his daughter Zinzi and nine other family members. The authorities had never before approved such an extended family visit.

But on Friday, three days before the gathering was to take place, Mr. Mandela requested through his wife that the visit be canceled. He said he did not want to accept favors from the Government.

"Nelson Is a Victor"

Very few South Africans, black or white, know Nelson Mandela. Most of those who know him best are in exile with the African National Congress.

"Nelson is a victor," said Oliver R. Tambo, the exiled president of the African National Congress and a former Johannesburg law partner of Mr. Mandela.

"He conquered the banning orders, he conquered his isolation," Mr. Tambo said in an interview in Lusaka, Zambia. "He is everywhere in the world. He conquered prison and now they are keeping him in jail because they are afraid of him."

Constant Harassment

When Mr. Mandela was moved from the Alcatraz-like Robben Island prison to the mainland Pollsmoor jail, for reasons which have never been fully explained, Mrs. Mandela was allowed to sit with him during visits. Today, the conditions in which he is held have improved somewhat from the early days on Robben Island.

He may receive 30 visits of 40 minutes each a year. He may write 52 letters a year. He may receive 52 letters, 12 birthday cards and 12 Christmas cards each year.

He may read local and foreign newspapers, listen to local radio stations and watch a television set, which he recently received.

President Mandela greets a former worker from Victor Verster Prison, where Mandela was held from 1988 to 1990.

Prisoners who were on the island with Mr. Mandela have spoken of the enormous respect he commanded from prisoners and prison officials and the influence that he held.

Called "Mr. Mandela"

"Warders called him Mandela, though most inmates are simply referred to by their prison numbers," said Thami Mkhwanazi, a journalist who spent three years on the island with Mr. Mandela. "I remember one sergeant in particular even calling him Mr. Mandela, unheard of on Robben Island."

Since 1985, Mr. Mandela has turned down offers from Mr. Botha for his release in exchange for renouncing violence as a political tool. But Mr. Botha is adamant that Mr. Mandela, by refusing to renounce violence, is his own jailer.

"The choice is his. All that is required of him now is that he should unconditionally reject violence as a political instrument, a norm which is respected in all civilized countries of the world," Mr. Botha said.

Mr. Mandela responded to Mr. Botha through a written statement read to an anti-apartheid meeting in 1985: "I cannot sell my birthright, nor am I prepared to sell the birthright of the people to be free."

53

In the 1980s, political pressure on the apartheid government increased, at home and abroad. In New York, a massive protest was held against apartheid and in support of Nelson Mandela.

THOUSANDS IN NEW YORK RALLY AGAINST APARTHEID
By Dennis Hevesi
January 15, 1986

From all over Manhattan—Harlem and East Harlem, Chelsea and Greenwich Village, the Lower East Side and the Upper West Side—thousands of New Yorkers in two columns, from north and south, streamed together yesterday onto the Great Lawn of Central Park to chant their opposition to apartheid.

There were young and old, black and white, some blind, some in wheelchairs. There was a contingent from New Jersey and a sprinkling from other states. Estimates by the police placed the crowd at 35,000, but organizers said 90,000 attended.

Tuz Mende, seventy-four years old, said she had planned her trip from San Francisco so she could be a part of the demonstration. Sounding a theme echoed by many at the rally, Mrs. Mende said her presence was a statement not just to the Government of South Africa, but to the United States Government as well.

"The policy of the Reagan Administration is very deceptive," she said. "It does not fully condemn the policies of South Africa. Any decent-thinking person knows that pressure has to be put on the American Government, on businesses and universities that do business with South Africa."

Antiapartheid demonstration in Central Park, New York, June 1986.

Bearing Photos

About 11:45 A.M., more than an hour before several speakers were scheduled to mount a 60-foot-wide stage, the first marchers from Harlem massed on the grass, just north of the Delacorte Theater, pressing against the wooden barricades. Some carried photos of Martin Luther King Jr., Malcolm X and Nelson Mandela, the imprisoned leader of the outlawed African National Congress.

"Free Mandela," they chanted. "Death to Apartheid." Draped across the stage was a red, yellow, green, black and blue banner that read: "End Apartheid Now. Remember Soweto." Tomorrow is the 10th anniversary of the uprising in Soweto, the black township outside of Johannesburg.

Alexis Deveaux, an official of the New York Anti-Apartheid Coordinating Council, which sponsored the rally, greeted the marchers, saying: "Believe me, the people of the world are listening to us today. The Reagan Administration is listening to us today."

Marching north through the park, demonstrators who had gathered at Dag Hammarskjold Plaza and other sites south of Central Park came onto the field, some with signs that read: "Stop Funding Murder. Stop Funding Apartheid."

Jackson Cites Fascism

Mpho Tutu, the daughter of Bishop Desmond M. Tutu of South Africa, told the crowd: "We are a whisper away from a civil war. We are waiting for the world to do what it ought to do to end apartheid. This is our last chance."

With a style that galvanized the emotions of the day, the Rev. Jesse Jackson intoned, "Fascism is a threat to the whole human race and cannot be isolated." He said that every moral and ethical imperative that was used to fight Hitler in Nazi Germany "must be applied to Botha and apartheid in South Africa."

But it was the crowd itself that made the most poignant expressions of protest. Hundreds waved banners and flags bearing slogans reading, "One Person, One Vote" and "Break the Chains in South Africa." And a blond boy of about 4, mounted on his father's shoulders, wore a yellow T-shirt that said, "End Apartheid Now."

54

Winnie Mandela lived in the international limelight. Her years of persecution and isolation helped turn Winnie into a brutal and bitter woman and a liability to the ANC.

WINNIE MANDELA'S RISE AND FALL
By Emma Gilbey
April 4, 1992

The unraveling of the old order was the undoing of one of its most passionate adversaries. In the end, unable to adjust to change, Winnie Mandela could no longer be a hopeful symbol of the future, remaining instead a painful symptom of the past.

When Nelson Mandela announced yesterday that he and his wife had agreed to separate, it was the closing act of South Africa's lengthy drama of tyranny, fear, bloodshed and death. Mrs. Mandela, the champion of liberation, is headed toward the wings.

When did the end begin? Some say as early as the imprisonment of her husband in 1962, when she was a mother in her 20s struggling to deal with two girls and the burdens of activism. Her father knew what she was in for when he warned her on her wedding day in 1959 that she was marrying not the man but the struggle.

In the years that followed, the upheavals in her life reflected the country's strife. The Government imprisoned her, at one time holding her in solitary confinement for over a year. She was tortured, subjected to house arrest, kept under surveillance and eventually banished to Brandfort, a remote town in the Orange Free State.

Some believe it was her nine years of exile that set her adrift. And it was then, suffering from what must have been paralyzing loneliness, that she

Nelson Mandela with his wife, Winnie, on his release from prison, February 11, 1990.

began to drink heavily. The formation of Mandela United—her ruthless street gang—on her return to Soweto in 1986 caused the leaders of the liberation movement to distance themselves from her. That separation grew wider in May when she was convicted in the abduction and assault of four young men in Soweto, the youngest of whom was subsequently found murdered. This was the mother of the nation. That she could be associated with harming a child was untenable.

Freed on bail for a year now and awaiting a still unscheduled appeal, Mrs. Mandela has managed to retain significant power among the country's youth, who admire her militancy. But in the minds of many in the African National Congress, she became a liability. Flaunting a lover twenty-nine years her junior, she has been seen drunk, often disorderly.

Somewhere on the road to freedom the worst nightmare of oppression became a reality, as she, the oppressed, became a powerful oppressor in the black community. Yet no one succeeded in stopping her—if anyone tried. No one forced her to seek help, before or after Mr. Mandela was freed. The great reunion between her and her husband—lasting a mere 22 months—turned out to be little more than a romantic fantasy. Shortly before Christmas, Nelson Mandela, busy negotiating for the new South Africa, having promoted and protected his wife, moved out of their house.

Two weeks ago one of her two co-defendants confessed to having lied at last year's trial. Then, on Sunday, her driver claimed that instead of being away from home at the time of the kidnapping, Mrs. Mandela had initiated and participated in the crime and its cover-up. In addition, she had ordered him to dispose of the body of the murdered youth.

When it looked as if Nelson Mandela would become personally tarnished by his wife's scandals, pressure for him to announce their separation became overwhelming. When word leaked out that he had tried to have a negative story about her suppressed—hardly the act of someone fighting for a democratic society—a formal split seemed inevitable. That Nelson Mandela could be disgraced because of his wife was out of the question for A.N.C. leaders, who were well aware that what damaged the couple damaged the A.N.C.

Political expediency ended the relationship between the two—as it had in effect when Nelson Mandela went to prison thirty years ago. As family lawyers were asking the news media to respect the couple's privacy, Congress leaders were secretly telling reporters they could write what they liked about their leader's wife. It was open season on Winnie Mandela.

In the end, then, there may be no room for tyranny or scandal in the new South Africa, but there is little room for compassion, either.

65

The murder of Chris Hani, a popular leader of the Communist Party, caused an outpouring of anger.

A BLACK LEADER IN SOUTH AFRICA IS SLAIN AND A WHITE IS ARRESTED
By Bill Keller
Johannesburg, April 10, 1993

Chris Hani, the leader of the South African Communist Party and the most popular militant in the African National Congress, was shot and killed in the driveway of his home today, casting another anxious gloom over the country's transition to majority rule.

The police said they had arrested a 40-year-old white man, identified as Januzu Jakub Waluz, whose car license number was taken down by Mr. Hani's neighbors as he fled the racially mixed neighborhood. They declined to say if he was known to have any political affiliation.

The Sunday Times of Johannesburg, in a story prepared for its Sunday issue, said the suspect was a Polish immigrant with violently anti-Communist views and "close links" to a militant white nationalist group, the Afrikaner Resistance Movement.

Blow to Negotiations

The assassination of Mr. Hani is a staggering blow to the African National Congress as it tries to negotiate the end of white rule. With his credentials as an anti-apartheid guerrilla leader and his charismatic appeal to angry young blacks, Mr. Hani gave the Congress credibility among its most disaffected constituents.

Before being elected General Secretary of the Communist Party in 1991, Mr. Hani was the chief of staff of the Congress's military wing, Spear of the Nation. He remained on the Congress's governing board, and took part in the political negotiations on the transition to majority rule as part of a congress-led alliance.

Judging by public opinion polls and by votes at congress conventions, Mr. Hani, 50, was second only to Nelson Mandela in popularity among blacks, and he was on most short lists of candidates to eventually succeed Mr. Mandela, the 74-year-old president of the congress.

Without Mr. Hani, it will be harder to sell any compromise in the black townships and to galvanize young voters for the first all-race elections, expected to take place in about a year.

Mr. Mandela issued a statement full of grief but containing no hint of recrimination. He appealed "with all the authority at my command" for followers to remain calm and forgo reprisals.

Tonight, state television interrupted its programming for Mr. Mandela's brief tribute to Mr. Hani, an unprecedented move that underscored the Government's eagerness to defuse tensions from the killing. To many white South Africans, Mr. Hani has long symbolized the militant Bolshevism they feared would come to power on Mr. Mandela's coattails.

President F. W. de Klerk, who has often used Mr. Hani and the Communist Party as favorite bogies, said the killing would "undermine the

Chris Hani's funeral, April 19, 1993.

work of people of good will from all political persuasions who strove for a peaceful future."

"He and I were at opposite poles of the political debate," Mr. de Klerk said. "But we were both prepared to resolve the problems of our country through the process of peaceful negotiations."

Violence erupted in the months leading up to the first free election while Mandela and de Klerk negotiated a new constitution.

39 IN SOUTH AFRICA DIE IN A MASSACRE
By Bill Keller
Boipatong, South Africa, June 18, 1992

Mobs of armed attackers shot and hacked their way through this black township and an adjoining squatter camp on Wednesday night, leaving at least 39 people dead and delivering a jolt to negotiations on South Africa's political future.

Witnesses said today that the attackers were Zulu-speaking men who had been brought to the scene and assisted in the seemingly random massacre by the South African police. The police heatedly denied involvement.

The victims, in what was one of the largest township massacres ever carried out, included a nine-month-old child impaled through the head and found lying in the arms of his dead mother, a pregnant woman riddled with gunshot and knife wounds, and several elderly men and women shot or axed as they tried to flee their homes.

Dozens more were wounded, including eight children who were in critical condition tonight in the wards of Sebokeng Hospital.

After touring Boipatong, 35 miles south of Johannesburg, and Slovo Park, the squatter settlement, Cyril Ramaphosa, the secretary general of the African National Congress, told reporters this afternoon, "We have never seen an incident as horrific as the one we have witnessed here."

De Klerk Blamed

"We charge de Klerk and his Government with complicity in the slaughter that has taken place in this area," Mr. Ramaphosa said, referring to President F. W. de Klerk. He added that the incident "could very well lead to the negotiating process being derailed."

The congress is the Government's principal negotiating partner in talks aimed at creating a transition government to draw up a new constitution and a nonracial political system. The congress announced on Tuesday a campaign of rallies and strikes aimed at breaking an impasse in the talks and speeding enfranchisement of the country's black majority.

Mr. Ramaphosa suggested that the police, together with allies from the conservative Zulu-based Inkatha Freedom Party, had sponsored the massacre, hoping to spread terror through the townships and discredit the congress's protest campaign. Inkatha denied any involvement.

67

After months of negotiations, Nelson Mandela, president of the ANC, South African president F. W. de Klerk, and eighteen other leaders approve a new constitution.

SOUTH AFRICAN PARTIES ENDORSE CONSTITUTION GRANTING RIGHTS TO ALL
By Bill Keller
Johannesburg, Thursday, November 18, 1993

South Africa's main political antagonists this morning concluded their grand bargain to end white dominion, endorsing a new constitution that tries to balance majority rule with safeguards to reassure whites and other minorities.

In the cavern of a suburban convention center, black and white leaders renounced the racist past and embraced a bill of rights promising South Africans freedoms of speech, movement and political activity and other liberties that in the past were reserved mainly for whites.

Among the vestiges of apartheid abolished today in an exuberant final round of compromise were the 10 self-governing homelands invented by apartheid as reservations for the country's blacks. These desolate black homelands and their autocratic little governments are to disappear when the new constitution takes effect, immediately after elections in April.

Ominously missing from the gathering where Nelson Mandela, President F. W. de Klerk and 18 other leaders approved the documents were the Zulu-based Inkatha Freedom Party and an array of white separatist groups, which have threatened to boycott elections and hinted at insurrection.

Speaking in English, Xhosa and Afrikaans to dramatize the new spirit of reconciliation, Mr. Mandela told his country's angry minorities, "You are welcome in this country," but warned that "Democracy has no place for talk of civil war."

Mr. de Klerk said the document fulfilled his vision of a new South Africa "where freedom, peace and justice could walk hand in hand."

"New and Equal Opportunities"

"My vision was a new South Africa where men and women of all races would have new and equal opportunities to develop the talents God gave them," he said. "It was on this day that we laid the foundation for a new South African nation."

The agreement ended seven years of fitful negotiating that began in Mr.

Mandela's jail cell, and became over the last two years a formal diplomatic minuet involving up to 26 political parties and Government bodies.

Most of that effort was directed at finding a formula that would calm whites who fear for their safety and property under a mainly black government, without giving minorities the power to paralyze democracy.

The 142-page constitution, which is to serve as South Africa's supreme law until an elected assembly can write a permanent version, is laden with assurances. It promises minority parties seats in a 27-member Cabinet for the first five years, protects the jobs and pensions of white soldiers and civil servants, delegates important powers to provincial governments, and backs up a long list of "fundamental rights" with a powerful constitutional court.

De Klerk Yields on Major Issue

But for all the built-in checks and balances, in the end, the party that wins the election wins most of the power. In a final recognition of that hard reality, the Government today surrendered on an important dispute over how much power minority parties will have in the Cabinet.

Until the last moment, Mr. de Klerk held out for a formula that would oblige the president to obtain two-thirds support in the Cabinet on major issues. The final version only requires the President to consult the Cabinet in a "consensus-seeking spirit" before making decisions.

South Africa's new constitution was signed in George Thabe Stadium, Sharpeville, on December 10, 1996. This member of the crowd holds a poster in reference to the Sharpeville massacre of 1960.

In April, voters, including for the first time the 75 percent of the population that is black, will cast a single ballot for the party they want to represent them in the new national Parliament and in provincial legislatures.

The Parliament—a 400-seat Assembly and a 90-seat Senate—will make laws and simultaneously craft a permanent constitution. It will also choose a President, a position that Mr. Mandela is widely expected to win.

There will be at least two Deputy Presidents, one of them possibly Mr. de Klerk, and a Cabinet including ministers from any party that gets at least 5 percent of the popular vote.

The first post-apartheid government is to serve for five years, although it is expected to complete the permanent constitution within two years.

The President will also name an 11-member constitutional court, drawing from a list of candidates approved by an impartial commission.

The country is to be divided into nine new provinces, each of which would run their own police, schools, hospitals and other services. They would also select the members of the Senate, which is envisioned as the defender of provincial interests.

But ultimately provinces are bound by the constitution and laws of South Africa. Their powers fall far short of the autonomy demanded by Inkatha and white Afrikaner nationalists, who had hoped to create provincial bastions largely free of central control.

For Afrikaners, this means there will be no white "volkstaat" in which they can run their own affairs. For Inkatha, it means that even if Mr. Buthelezi wins provincial elections in his eastern stronghold of Natal, he must defer to a central Government run by Mr. Mandela's group.

The constitution repeals the South African laws that granted independence to four black homelands—Transkei, Ciskei, Bophuthatswana and Venda. Although some of these homelands may resist the loss of their independence, Government lawyers said that once South African laws are repealed, the homelands will lose legal standing because no other country recognizes their independence.

For all the elaborate legalisms of the new South African constitution, it is in essence a passionate reaction against apartheid by negotiators, many of whom experienced the jails, tortures and exile of the old order.

List of Basic Rights

The list of fundamental rights includes not only such democratic basics as free speech and fair trials, but also guarantees that reflect the abuses of the recent past: a specific prohibition against torture, a promise that people can live where they choose, an assurance that no one may be stripped of his citizenship, and three pages limiting the President's power to declare a state of emergency, a favorite apartheid-era tool for crushing dissent.

The charter forbids discrimination not only by race, but by sex, sexual orientation, physical disability or age.

The single most contentious issue over the last two years was how the next constitution will be drafted.

The African National Congress worried that if the process was too cumbersome a minority could stall it to death. The Government feared that if it was too easy the A.N.C. could write a constitution on its own.

The final formula was an elaborate compromise. If the constitution-writers cannot agree on a new document by a two-thirds vote, then the draft will be put to a popular referendum requiring 60 percent approval. If that fails, an entirely new parliament will be elected and may enact a constitution with a 60 percent majority.

The new interim constitution, which is to replace a constitution in effect since 1984, must be ratified by the existing Parliament, a formality expected by mid-December.

73

Despite violence leading up to election day, long lines of voters participate in the first democratic election in the new South Africa.

AFTER 300 YEARS, BLACKS VOTE IN SOUTH AFRICA
By Francis X. Clines
Johannesburg, Wednesday, April 27, 1994

Throngs of elderly and infirm voters came forward in the predawn Tuesday to sweep aside three centuries of white racist rule and euphorically open the first fully democratic elections in South Africa.

Three out of four were newly enfranchised black voters, the vanguard of the nation's long-oppressed black majority, who patiently crowded polling booths and celebrated the power of the ballot in their ascension from the hard subjugation of apartheid.

"I don't want the whites to go away," said 80-year-old Christina Vanqa, a spry black woman, recently retired as a maid, who happily lined up at 5 A.M. to cast the first national ballot of a lifetime freighted with racist deprivation. "We want to stay with them and build South Africa together."

The new political majority's determination was signaled across the nation by the sight of the old and the sick arriving with wheelchair, crutch and cane, and in the arms of loved ones, too, to cast the first ballots in three days of voting.

Their efforts are to produce a new government of power-sharing under a constitution, rooted in human rights guarantees, that took effect at midnight. New national flags were readied across the land and were run up at midnight.

"Today is a day like no other before it," declared Nelson Mandela, the leader and hero of the blacks' liberation struggle, who is expected to be elected the first President of the reforming nation, four years after he was freed from 27 years of apartheid imprisonment. "Voting in our first free and fair election has begun. Today marks the dawn of our freedom."

Thousands of expatriates voted overseas after years of waiting out apartheid's demise. Here, the nation seemed to pause and sigh as if on a long-denied holiday, collective pride fairly palpable as the business of universal voting was finally undertaken before the eyes of a world that was so recently scornful of South Africa.

Although the first day was set aside for voters who might otherwise be overwhelmed by the larger crowds expected today and Thursday, there were some difficulties.

Ballot shortages and other technical problems, combined with the first-day crush, sparked calls to extend the voting period. But election officials insisted they would manage the vast undertaking, which reaches from the high-security residential enclaves of the white elite down to the meanest squatter camps of the black underclass.

President-in-Waiting

While most voting is to come on the second and third days, and Mr. Mandela is not expected to be elected by the new Parliament until May 10, he was being treated as President-in-waiting Tuesday at a crowded news conference. He handily fielded questions on foreign policy and passionately saluted the first wave of voters for ignoring the deadly pre-election bomb blasts of diehard opponents of the new South Africa.

In some parts of the rugged national landscape, pockets of white separatists boycotted the voting, maintaining demands for their own homeland. But history seemed to ravel around them in the long lines of blacks finally stepping up to the ballot boxes.

Most of the 5 million whites seemed ready to accept the rise of the 30 million blacks. The elaborate power-sharing government was worked out by Mr. Mandela and President F. W. de Klerk, the leader of the National Party, which finally moderated itself after more than four harsh decades.

What They Are Voting For

"I feel a sense of achievement," Mr. de Klerk said Tuesday, escorting his 89-year-old mother, Corrie, to the polls. "My plan has been put into operation." He leads his ticket and expects to be a vice president.

The procedure allots two vice presidencies, and cabinet representation to all parties who win a 5 percent share of the vote. A 400-seat National Assembly will be chosen according to each party's share. The 90-seat Senate is to be elected by provincial legislatures. A blitz of 19 parties, mixing not just race but religion and fringe causes as well, is greeting the voters.

Secondary ballots cover the nine newly drawn provinces, where regional parliaments and premiers are to be elected. Counting begins Friday, with the results supposed to be announced as early as the weekend. There were no immediate estimates on the number of votes cast Tuesday.

Doubts that the voting process can manage the task grew in the first hours.

No Zulu Party on Some Ballots

The problems included the last-minute insertion of Inkatha, Mangosuthu G. Buthelezi's Zulu nationalist party, on all ballots, using stickers, which were missing in some cases. Officials also wondered whether as many as a million late-registering Zulu voters could ever be accommodated by the 450 ballot boxes promised by the Independent Election Commission.

The only violence reported was the burning of two trucks carrying ballot equipment; no one was injured.

Bomb blasts on Sunday and Monday killed 21 people in attempts to intimidate voters. The police have been questioning at least three men, arresting

Young ANC supporters in Johannesburg during the campaign for South African presidential elections, April 23, 1994.

them under a draconian statute still on the books from the apartheid era. A fourth man, detained earlier, was released. White militants were suspected in the blasts, but no one has been charged yet.

For all the reconciliation, the election campaign was rugged. The National Party reached out to the large mixed-race and Indian minorities, arguing that black majorities have failed to ever show they can govern effectively in Africa.

Mr. Mandela, dismissing this as racist politicking, appealed for a multi-racial mandate so he can get on with national reconstruction and fulfill the high aspirations demonstrated in today's voting throngs.

"What I feel is beyond words," he declared. "I am excited that the many years of struggle in which our people have been involved are now going to be rewarded."

73

Nelson Mandela celebrates his victory and de Klerk graciously concedes defeat in the historic election.

MANDELA PROCLAIMS A VICTORY: SOUTH AFRICA IS 'FREE AT LAST!'
By Bill Keller
Johannesburg, May 2, 1994

With a dignity that owed nothing to defeat, Frederik Willem de Klerk, the last white ruler in Africa, tonight conceded his presidency to Nelson Rolihlahla Mandela.

"Mr. Mandela has walked a long road, and now stands at the top of the hill," said Mr. de Klerk of the man he freed after 27 years in prison, and with whom he negotiated the surrender of white power. "As he contemplates the next hill, I hold out my hand to Mr. Mandela in friendship and in cooperation."

Mr. Mandela later seized his election mandate with matching grace before a rapturous crowd in a Johannesburg hotel ballroom. He welcomed Mr. de Klerk and other political rivals as partners in a new Government of national unity.

"I stand here before you filled with deep pride and joy," Mr. Mandela said.

"Pride in the ordinary, humble people of this country—you have shown such a calm, patient determination to reclaim this country as your own. And joy that we can loudly proclaim from the rooftops: free at last!"

Acknowledging his political collaboration with Mr. de Klerk, Mr. Mandela said, "I also want to congratulate him for the many days, weeks and months and the four years that we have worked together, quarreled, addressed sensitive problems and at the end of our heated exchanges were able to shake hands and to drink coffee."

Black South Africans tonight poured into the streets of Soweto and Alexandra, lit the dim township streets with bonfires, danced and chanted Mr. Mandela's name in a triumphant delirium.

Speaking in a voice husky from a head cold, Mr. Mandela tonight implored his supporters to keep their celebrations "peaceful, respectful and disciplined, showing we are a people ready to assume the responsibilities of government," especially in those areas that did not vote for his party.

Among the leaders who had called to congratulate him on his victory, and with whom he expected to work in the future, Mr. Mandela named Mr. de Klerk and—to some disapproving murmurs from his audience—Gen. Constandt Viljoen, the leader of the white separatist front. He did not name Chief Buthelezi of Inkatha, although Chief Buthelezi later said he had phoned.

Any party polling 5 percent of the votes is entitled to a seat in the coalition Cabinet, though in his acceptance speech Mr. Mandela hinted strongly that he would also invite some parties that fell short of the threshhold to join the government anyway.

He suggested he would make an offer to the Pan Africanist Congress, the more militant rival liberation movement, which was winning a little more than 1 percent of the vote.

"I have got certain ideas," he said. "They have suffered together with us."

Composition of Cabinet

Details of the new Cabinet are to be negotiated in the coming days, but the new array is expected to include several holdovers from the de Klerk Government.

Mr. Mandela, who as president would have a veto over Cabinet appointments, said tonight he would not make room for anyone opposed to the African National Congress's social agenda, which calls for building a million houses in five years, a public works employment program, and free, compulsory education for all.

"If there are attempts on the part of anyone to undermine that program, there will be serious tensions in the government of national unity," he warned.

A Toast to the Future

After his speech rambled to a close with an unscripted invitation to foreign sports teams to come play in South Africa, Mr. Mandela toasted Mr. de Klerk and the new South Africa with a flute of sweet sparkling wine.

A choir of 70 voices erupted into a liberation song, and the 75-year-old patriarch danced stiffly across the stage, joined by his fellow congress leaders and an eclectic contingent of shimmying celebrities that included Coretta Scott King, wife of the American civil rights leader, and Kenneth Kaunda, the former president of Zambia.

Mr. de Klerk spoke to a sober and misty-eyed gathering of 300 of the party faithful in Pretoria.

Standing alongside his tearful wife, Marike, he pointedly reminded the world that he will not be in the government "at the whim of any person or any party" but by Constitutional right, and backed by a potent constituency that includes the civil service Mr. Mandela will inherit.

"Just as we could not rule South Africa effectively without the support of the A.N.C. and its supporters, no Government will be able to rule South Africa effectively without the support of the people and the institutions that I as your leader in the National Party represent," he said.

Bound by this mutual dependency, Mr. Mandela and Mr. de Klerk have led South Africa on a remarkable course from lethal racial confrontation through a negotiated revolution to a reconciliation many South Africans still regard with disbelief.

"Next Tuesday I shall lay down my responsibility as state president, secure in the knowledge that we have achieved what we set out to achieve four years and three months ago," Mr. de Klerk said, referring to the day in February 1990 when he ordered Mr. Mandela released from prison.

For one rare evening in their often contentious partnership, the two men were matched in their sense of the moment.

Mr. Mandela proclaimed this "a joyous night for the human spirit," and read an honor roll of fallen campaigners for racial equality in South Africa.

"After so many centuries, all South Africans are now free," said Mr. de Klerk, before concluding with the title of the liberation prayer that is now one of the country's two national anthems: "God bless Africa," he said. "Nkosi Sikelele iAfrika."

84

Established to learn the truth and promote healing, the Truth and Reconciliation Commission listens to thousands of statements concerning human rights violations under apartheid.

THE WITNESS
By Mark Gevisser
June 22, 1997

For more than a year now, South Africa has been exposed to daily revelations about its traumatic history. In hearing rooms all over the country, people have been telling their stories to the Truth and Reconciliation

Commission, established by an act of Parliament to promote "reconciliation" among the races and to coax the truth out about apartheid by offering amnesty to those willing to confess their crimes.

The commission has received 10,000 statements charging gross violations of human rights—murder and torture—and nearly 7,000 applications for amnesty. It has become, in a way, a national town meeting on South Africa's past. A black mother brings a handful of her murdered son's hair to the witness stand; she does not know where his body is. A woman tells about the morning she realized her missing husband, a prominent activist, was dead; the hearing-room audience rises spontaneously and begins singing the African National Congress's funeral hymn for dead soldiers: "What have we done? What have we really done?"

The witnesses weep often, and when Bishop Desmond Tutu is presiding, he often weeps with them. Those seeking amnesty, by contrast, recite their crimes in an affectless monotone: the legislation does not require them to show contrition. They seek amnesty only to avoid prosecution.

Several families of murdered activists, including that of Steve Biko, have tried to stop the commission's work because they say the amnesty system denies them their right to see justice done through a criminal trial. Bishop Tutu insists, however, that the process remains "the only alternative to Nuremberg on the one hand and amnesia on the other." And he reminds his listeners that because South Africa came to a negotiated settlement, Nuremberg-style prosecutions are not an option.

The commission's amnesty process has done one thing the criminal justice system could never have achieved: it has ferreted out the truth. "We want to forgive," said the teen-aged daughter of a murdered activist at the beginning of the hearings last year. "But we don't know who to forgive." She will soon: her father's murderers have applied for amnesty, and they will testify in September. In the next few months, the amnesty applications of senior-level apartheid politicians and security officials will be heard, and they will make a mockery of former President F. W. de Klerk's repeated assertion that the atrocities were the work of a few "bad eggs." When the commission hands its report to President Mandela next year, the hope is that the investigations will prove that the assassinations of black leaders and the widespread use of torture were sanctioned at the highest level of the state.

De Klerk has recently thrown the "reconciliation" process into jeopardy by refusing to cooperate with the commission and threatening to sue it for "not being impartial." How could it be otherwise when one side was fighting a just war and the other was not? The commission is impelled to look at human rights abuses on both sides: the government that imposed apartheid and the liberation movements that fought to eliminate it. But whether you use a moral or a literal scale, the crimes of the former far outweigh those of the latter. De Klerk's response is emblematic of most white South Africans, who have been shocked by the evidence ("We never knew!") but have never taken responsibility for the acts committed in their name. Truth, as all South Africans are discovering, is not the same as justice. They are also learning that its relationship to reconciliation is far more complex than they imagined.

Timeline

1652: Jan Van Riebeeck lands on Cape Peninsula as commander of the expedition of the Dutch East India Company. Over the next century, the Dutch conquer the native peoples, import slaves, and call themselves "Afrikaners."

Zulu chiefs, South Africa, 1888.

1811–1879: British and colonial forces push east, displacing Africans, conquering first the Xhosa people and then the Zulus.

1867: Miners discover diamonds at Kimberley.

pre-1650: Southern Africa is populated by hunter-gatherers known as San, pastoral herdsmen known as Khoikhoi, and Bantu-speaking farmer-herdsmen, the forebears of most modern South Africans.

1795: British take control of the Cape Province.

1835: Beginning of the Afrikaner Great Trek. Unhappy under British rule of the Cape, Africanized descendants of the Dutch head east and north in wagon trains.

1880–1881: First Boer War between British and Afrikaners.

The Great Trek.

July 18, 1918: Nelson Mandela is born as Rolihlahla Mandela in Mvezo, a village in the Eastern Cape region.

1927: Nelson's father dies. Nelson and his mother move into the Great Place, home of his cousin, the acting chief of the Thembu.

1936: Mandela moves to Healdtown, a larger Methodist school.

1925: Mandela begins school in Qunu and is given the name Nelson by his schoolteacher.

1934: Mandela is sent to Clarkebury, a Methodist boarding school.

1939: Mandela is admitted to the South African Native College.

Battle of Eland River, September 17, 1901.

1886: Gold is discovered near Johannesburg, starting a gold rush. Within a decade, the region becomes the largest gold-mining area in the world.

1899–1902: Second Boer War between Afrikaners and British. The British win but at a huge cost in lives.

1912: African National Congress is formed to promote the cause of racial equality.

1893: Mohandas K. Gandhi begins a campaign to overturn laws that discriminate against Indians in South Africa.

1910: British and Afrikaner colonists unite to form Union of South Africa.

1914: Gandhi returns to India, where he will eventually lead a successful movement for independence from Great Britain.

South Africa's first prime minister, Louis Botha, ca. 1912.

1941: Mandela leaves college in his second year and runs away from an arranged marriage. He arrives in Soweto.

1944: Mandela marries Evelyn Mase.
1944: Mandela, Tambo, and Sisulu form the ANC Youth League.

1949: The Prohibition of Mixed Marriages Act.
1949: Mandela, Tambo, and Sisulu take over the ANC.

1943: Mandela joins the African National Congress.

1948: The National Party wins elections on a platform of strict separation of the races set out to implement apartheid.

1950: The Suppression of Communism Act.
1950: The Population Registration Act.
1950: The Group Areas Act.

National Party leader Daniel Malan.

Mandela addresses the ANC.

Bantu Education Act leads to empty classes.

Wedding of Nelson and Winnie Mandela.

1953: Reservation of Separate Amenities Act.
1953: Bantu Education Act.
1953: Mandela argues that the ANC should change tactics from peaceful civil disobedience to armed insurrection.

1958: Mandela marries Nomzamo Winifred Madikizela (Winnie).

1951: Bantu Authorities Act

1952: Mandela opens the first black law partnership in South Africa.
1952: The ANC sends the government an ultimatum demanding a repeal of major apartheid laws and threatening a national campaign of nonviolent resistance.

1956: The ANC organizes a conference of opposition groups to adopt a declaration of principles called the Freedom Charter.

March 21, 1960: Sharpeville massacre. Police kill sixty-nine peaceful protesters. Government bans ANC and other groups, which in turn adopt armed struggle.

Mandela released from prison.

1985: Mandela reaches out to the minister of justice, Kobie Coetsee, proposing that they begin negotiations. The two men begin secret talks in July 1986.

December 1988: Mandela is moved to a warden's cottage at Victor Verster Prison. Negotiations with the government intensify.

February 11, 1990: Nelson Mandela is released from Victor Verster Prison.

1982: Mandela is transferred to Pollsmoor, a prison on the mainland.

June 14, 1986: A bomb planted by Spear of the Nation explodes outside of a bar in Durban. Three women are killed and sixty-nine others are wounded.

February 2, 1990: F. W. de Klerk announces the release of all political prisoners and unbanning of antiapartheid organizations; state of emergency ends.

December 21, 1991: The Convention for a Democratic South Africa (CODESA)—including the government and opposition parties—begins negotiations aimed at creating a new constitution to end white rule.

Police tear-gas a student gathering, 1987.

Act of sabotage by the "Spear of the Nation," 1963.

Rioter in Soweto, June 21, 1976.

March, 1961: Court dismisses treason charges against Mandela and others.
1961: Spear of the Nation, ANC's new rebel army, formed. Mandela named first commander.

1963: Rivonia Trial. Mandela is brought back to Pretoria to stand trial, along with Walter Sisulu and seven others, for conspiracy to overthrow the state. The defendants attempt to make the case a trial of the apartheid system.

1970s: Protests, strikes, and acts of sabotage begin to shake the order of apartheid.

1980s: Unrest in black townships makes the country difficult to govern; condemnation of the outside world, including economic sanctions.

August 5, 1962: Nelson Mandela is arrested for inciting unrest and leaving the country without a passport, and in November is sentenced to five years in prison. After six months in Pretoria jail, he is sent to Robben Island Prison.

June 12, 1964: Along with other defendants, Mandela receives life sentence. He returns to Robben Island.

1976: Soweto student uprising, beginning with protest of required study of Afrikaans.

April 26–28, 1994: Elections for a parliament and regional legislatures, the first in which the black majority votes.
May 6, 1994: National Assembly convenes in Cape Town and elects Nelson Mandela the first president of the new South Africa.
May 10, 1994: Mandela is inaugurated as president.

June 17, 1992: A nighttime massacre in Biopatong township by Inkatha supporters prompts Mandela to break off formal talks with the government for nine months.

1998: Mandela marries Graca Machel.

2005: Mandela reveals his son died of AIDS; continues his campaign for AIDS/HIV awareness.

April 10, 1993: Chris Hani, a popular young leader of the South African Communist Party, is murdered by a white nationalist.
November 18, 1993: Negotiators agree on a new constitution, outlining fundamental rights in the new South Africa.
December 10, 1993: Mandela and de Klerk are jointly awarded the Nobel Peace Prize.

1997: Robben Island is made a museum.

1999: Mandela succeeded by Thabo Mbeki.

2013: Nelson Mandela dies, December 5, 2013.

Mandela and his successor, Mbeki.

Source Notes

Although this book grew out of my own experiences and the archives of *The New York Times*, I am indebted to several books and other references.

Mandela's autobiography, *Long Walk to Freedom*, is almost as fascinating as the man himself. His memories of his childhood, his young manhood, and his time in prison are rich, and unlike many heroic figures, he writes about himself with a sense of humor and humility. I also made use of two well-researched accounts of his life—*Nelson Mandela: A Biography*, by Martin Meredith, and *Mandela: The Authorized Biography*, by Anthony Sampson.

For an understanding of Winnie Mandela, I turned to *The Lady: The Life and Times of Winnie Mandela*, by Emma Gilbey, who is now Emma Gilbey Keller. (You could say I am married to South Africa.)

Leonard Thompson's *A History of South Africa* is the indispensable account of that country from the time before the whites arrived to modern day. The Leonard Thompson quote in Chapter 1 was taken from this source.

A brilliant account of life under apartheid is *Move Your Shadow: Black and White in South Africa*, by Joseph Lelyveld. He was twice the *New York Times* correspondent in South Africa and went on to be the paper's executive editor—also twice.

Here are some other resources I found useful:

An interesting video account of Mandela's life, including interviews with him and many of the key figures in his life, is *The Long Walk of Nelson Mandela*, produced by Frontline for PBS. Tapes and DVDs are no longer available from PBS, but you may find a copy at your local library. You can see summaries, view pictures, and read a transcript of the show at the PBS website (www.pbs.org/wgbh/pages/frontline/shows/mandela/).

The Nelson Mandela National Museum website (www.nelsonmandela museum.org.za) contains background information and pictures of his childhood villages.

The Robben Island Museum website (www.robben-island.org.za)

includes interesting information, pictures, and maps of the island.

Several points on the timeline were taken from "A Country's Road to Democracy," published April 24, 1994, in *The New York Times*.

The following articles appeared as illustration or text:

"Verdict in South Africa." *The New York Times*, June 14, 1964.

"How Diamonds Were Found in South Africa." *The New York Times*, July 28, 1878.

"Millions Esteemed Gandhi as a Saint." *The New York Times*, January 31, 1948.

Wren, Christopher S. "Mandela Lives Without Regrets, His Son Reports." *The New York Times*, December 21, 1989.

Ingalls, Leonard. "South Africa: Rising Racial Tensions." *The New York Times*, March 26, 1960.

"What Mandela Wants: Statements at His '64 Trial." *The New York Times*, February 11, 1990.

Battersby, John D. "Mandela, 70, Captivates Even Those Who Jail Him." *The New York Times*, July 17, 1988.

Hevesi, Dennis. "Thousands in New York Rally Against Apartheid." *The New York Times*, January 15, 1986.

Gilbey, Emma. "Winnie Mandela's Rise and Fall." *The New York Times*, April 4, 1992.

Keller, Bill. "A Black Leader in South Africa Is Slain and a White Is Arrested." *The New York Times*, April 10, 1993.

Keller, Bill. "39 in South Africa Die in a Massacre." *The New York Times*, June 18, 1992.

Keller, Bill. "South African Parties Endorse Constitution Granting Rights to All." *The New York Times*, November 18, 1993.

Clines, Francis X. "After 300 Years, Blacks Vote in South Africa." *The New York Times*, April 27, 1994.

Keller, Bill. "Mandela Proclaims a Victory: South Africa Is 'Free At Last!'" *The New York Times*, May 2, 1994.

Gevisser, Mark. "The Witness." *The New York Times*, June 22, 1997.

Acknowledgments

Whatever I know of South Africa I know mostly thanks to hundreds of South Africans, of all races and outlooks, who let me into their lives while I was the Johannesburg bureau chief of *The New York Times* from 1992 to 1995. They included shack-dwellers and mine workers, ministers and schoolteachers, farmers and bankers, township thugs and militant racists, journalists and actors, activists of all persuasions, and—on several occasions—Nelson Mandela.

Joe Lelyveld wrote unforgettable accounts of South Africa as a correspondent and author, and he spent some time traveling with me in South Africa. But my main debt to Joe is that, as a top editor of *The New York Times*, he sent me in his footsteps. I had the best support a reporter could want from the foreign desk headed by Bernie Gwertzman. I learned a lot from other *Times* colleagues who worked in Africa, and I have kept up with South Africa through the fine work of several successors—Suzanne Daley, Donald McNeil, Rachel Swarns, Michael Wines, and Sharon LaFraniere. During my time in South Africa, I had many wise traveling companions, including reporters for other newspapers, but the most valuable one was photojournalist Greg Marinovich. Greg brought not only a great eye but a gift of gab that sometimes got us out of tricky situations. During the exhilarating elections of 1994, I had reinforcements. Amy Waldman signed on as my assistant, and I like to think the experience helped rocket her to a great journalistic career. A number of *New York Times* journalists joined me at various periods, bringing fresh eyes and good company: Frank Clines, Isabel Wilkerson, Donatella Lorch, Tony Lewis, and Ken Noble. Ozier Mohamed, a great photographer and great companion, was with me on the Mandela campaign, including the one-thousand-mile election day flight around South Africa.

I'm grateful to Deirdre Langeland, who edited with respect for both the story and its readership.

Above all, I thank my family for making it all worthwhile: my son, Tom, who saw his first lion and his first ocean in South Africa; my daughters, Molly and Alice; and, always, my wife, Emma.

Picture Credits

The publisher would like to thank the following for permission to reproduce their material. Every care has been taken to trace copyright holders. However, if there have been unintentional omissions, we apologize and will, if informed, endeavor to make corrections in any future edition.

Cover: Corbis/Hans Gedda/Sygma.

Pages 1: Corbis/Peter Turnley; 2–3: Corbis/epa/Scott Applewhite; 4–5: Ozier Muhammad/*The New York Times*; 6: Corbis/epa/Jon Hrusa; 9: Corbis/Gallo Images; 10–11: Corbis/Louise Gubb; 12: Corbis/Louise Gubb; 13: Corbis/Charles/O'Rear; 14: Corbis/epa/Jon Hrusa; 15: Corbis; 16: Getty/Mansell/Time & Life Pictures; 18–19: Corbis/Underwood & Underwood; 20: Corbis/Hulton; 21: Corbis/Underwood & Underwood; 23: Corbis/Hulton; 26: Corbis Bettmann; 28: Corbis/Tony Aruzza; 30: Corbis/Gallo Images; 32: W.E.B. du Bois Photos/ University of Massachusetts; 33: Bailey's African History Archive; 34: Bailey's African History Archive; 36: Corbis/Reuters; 38: Getty/Grey Villet/Time & Life Pictures; 39: PA Photos/AP; 40: PA Photos/AP; 41: Getty/Hulton; 42–43: PA Photos/AP; 44: Getty/Hulton; 45: Bailey's African History Archive; 46: Corbis/Jean Miele; 49: Bailey's African History Archive; 50: Corbis/Bettmann; 51: Getty/AFP; 52–53: Corbis/William Campbell/Sygma; 55: Corbis/Antoine Gyori/Sygma; 57: Corbis/Peter Turnley; 60–61: Corbis/Greg Marvinovich/Sygma; 62: Corbis/Peter Turnley; 64: Getty/William Campbell/Sygma; 65: Corbis/Louise Gubb; 67: PA Photos/AP; 68: Ozier Muhammad/*The New York Times*; 69: Ozier Muhammad/*The New York Times*; 70: PA Photos/AP; 71: PA Photos/AP; 72: Ozier Muhammad/*The New York Times*; 74: PA Photos/AP; 75: Ozier Muhammad/*The New York Times*; 76: Ozier Muhammad/*The New York Times*; 78: Bailey's African History Archive; 79: Corbis/Anthony Bolante/Sygma; 80: PA Photos/AP; 82–83: PA Photos/AP; 84: Corbis/Herve Collart/Sygma; 85: Getty/Trevor Samson/AFP; 89: Mary Evans Picture Library; 90: Corbis/Bettmann; 93: Corbis/Bettmann; 96: Bailey's African History Archive; 99: Corbis/Louise Gubb; 102–103: Dith Pran/*The New York Times*; 104: Corbis/Sygma; 107: Corbis/Patrick Robert/Sygma; 110: Corbis/Charles O'Rear; 114: Corbis/David Brauchi/Sygma; 118: Corbis/Bettmann (t), Mary Evans Picture Library (b); 119: Art Archive/Ellen Tweedy (t), Mary Evans Picture Library (c), Getty/Hulton (bc), Bailey's African History Archive (br); 120: Bailey's African History Archive (tl), Getty/AFP (tr), PA Photos/AP (cr), PA Photos/AP (bl); 121: Bailey's African History Archive (tl), Corbis/Gideon Mendel (tr), Getty Hrvoje Polan (b).

Index